Crying Scarlet Tears

My journey through self-harm

Sophie Scott

MONARCH
BOOKS

Oxford, UK & Grand Rapids, Michigan, USA

Copyright © 2008 by Sophie Scott.

The right of Sophie Scott to be identified as author of this work has been asserted by her in accordance with the Copyright, Designs and Patents Act 1988.

First published in the UK in 2008 by Monarch Books
(a publishing imprint of Lion Hudson plc),
Wilkinson House, Jordan Hill Road, Oxford OX2 8DR
Tel: +44 (0) 1865 302750   Fax: +44 (0) 1865 302757
Email: monarch@lionhudson.com
www.lionhudson.com

ISBN: 978-1-85424-818-3 (UK)
ISBN: 978-0-8254-6169-9 (USA)

Distributed by:
UK: Marston Book Services Ltd, PO Box 269, Abingdon, Oxon OX14 4YN;
USA: Kregel Publications, PO Box 2607, Grand Rapids, Michigan 49501.

Unless otherwise stated, Scripture quotations are taken from the Holy Bible, New International Version, © 1973, 1978, 1984 by the International Bible Society. Used by permission of Hodder and Stoughton Ltd. All rights reserved.

Every effort has been made to trace the copyright holders of material quoted in this book. If any item has been incorrectly attributed, please inform the publisher for correction in subsequent printings.

This book has been printed on paper and board independently certified as having come from sustainable forests.

British Library Cataloguing Data
A catalogue record for this book is available from the British Library.

Printed and bound in Wales by Creative Print & Design.

For all my friends on the BUS.

CONTENTS

ACKNOWLEDGMENTS

I would like to thank Carter, whom I love with all my heart, for being such a rock of support to me, and Melody and Harry for the amazing way they've helped and encouraged me to write this book. I would also like to thank all my friends at St Paul's Church and at school and university for helping me through the years. And mostly I would like to thank God for never giving up on me.

PREFACE

I am a real person, and this is my true story. All the names in this book, however, have been changed, and some unimportant details have been altered. This is not because I am afraid or ashamed, but simply to protect members of my family. Honesty is always a good thing when it is needed, but pursuing honesty for honesty's sake without taking all the consequences into consideration can be harmful.

THE DAY IT ALL BEGAN

Looking back on it, I still don't know why it happened that night. I realize now that it was going to begin at some point, but what I don't understand is why it was that day in particular that I started self-harming.

I'd had an average Wednesday at school: too much maths and sport, not enough English or art. I went to a suburban girls' high school which was incredibly academic. But even though I was not the smartest person there, I never felt criticized: the teachers were always encouraging the girls to do their best, however varied their 'best' was. The school had a friendly atmosphere, but as in all girls-only schools there were many catfights, and best friends became worst enemies within minutes. One incident that may have contributed to triggering the self-harm was a spat I had that day with my best friend, Davina.

Davina and I had been on-again, off-again best friends since I'd started attending the secondary school three years before. When I first met her we became very close very quickly, but she always seemed to have control of our friendship and I had to follow the 'rules'. Some days I would come to school and find her ignoring me, actually pretending I wasn't there for the whole day, if not longer. Other days she'd phone me as soon as I got home and insist on talking to me for hours. She'd often criticize various girls at the school who didn't live up to her interpretation of 'cool'. This day, she decided to gripe about Becky.

Becky was a quiet but kind girl with whom I'd talked many times. I'd always thought of her as a good person, so when Davina started saying horrible things about her I decided that I wouldn't stand for it. I told Davina I hated her slating people and that she was mean. I said it was typical of her, that she always did it, and that I wouldn't stand for it. I was harsh, too harsh.

She didn't say anything for a while. We both pretended to study. I could see tears falling onto her work, smudging the ink. I'd actually made her cry: something I'd never seen her do in the three years I'd known her. We stayed quiet for the whole of the lesson, and when the bell went for lunch she jumped up and hurried away from me. However, at the end of break she came back happy and cheerful, so we pretended the argument had never happened. In fact, by the end of the day we were giggling and messing around again as usual.

After school I came home and performed my daily chore of feeding the cats. I had two cats called Twinks and Tinker. Every day at four o'clock Tinker would leave my mum's lap to wait on the doorstep, then he'd run down the driveway to greet me when I came round the corner. I used to believe it was because he loved me and missed me, but in actual fact it was probably just because I was the one who fed him! After I'd made sure they were content with their bizarre concoction of canned beef and duck, I went into the living room and sat down with my mum. She was reading a trashy magazine which I'd tease her about every week. I used to say it was the same as her making fun of me for watching the Ricki Lake show, if not worse. She gave her customary excuse, which was that she only bought it for the crossword puzzles. I switched on the TV and watched some children's programmes before setting off to babysit a child I had sat for regularly in the past. It was his eighth birthday, and I was helping his parents look after a dozen screaming kids rampaging round an adventure playground. It was tiring work, but fantastic. I've always loved kids: there's something about their innocence, openness and honesty that grabs hold of me – even the naughty ones! After the party, we took the kids back to the boy's house and played more party games, fed the kids too much junk food and then sent them back to their own parents' houses so that they could throw up there if they needed to!

Afterwards, his parents drove me home to an empty house. My brother, three years older than me, was rarely at home in those days, choosing to congregate with friends rather than stay in and study for his A-level exams. Neither of us was disciplined to study. It felt as though I was forever being rebuked by teachers for not handing in homework. I can only remember once when I actually did hand in work on time, and I was accused of plagiarism! However, even though neither my brother nor I worked at school, we both did surprisingly well in our exams.

My parents were enjoying a night out with some friends. They had told me they'd be out, yet opening the door to a dark house filled me with a loneliness I hadn't expected. It wasn't unusual for me to be alone at home, but this time I felt something wasn't right. I didn't want to be by myself. It felt as if something bad was going to happen and I felt uncomfortable. To distract myself, I went to play with my cats for a while, dangling a piece of string over them both as they attacked it manically. After a few minutes I began to relax again, and everything seemed to return to normal.

Not bothering with my homework, as usual, I shoved a meal in the microwave and sat down to watch a video. After eating, I went upstairs to take a shower. Our bathroom was constantly messy. On the shelf there were five cups holding about twenty old toothbrushes that nobody used but nobody threw away, and although the floor was tiled it looked carpeted thanks to the numerous discarded towels that nobody picked up.

I can't remember thinking about anything in particular while showering. The whole day had seemed pretty regular so far. But then I got out of the shower, and before I'd even dried myself I picked up a wooden coat-hanger and hit my leg with it. No thoughts or emotions seemed to go through my mind: it felt so ordinary, so mundane. I looked down at the faint red mark it had left on my calf and I liked what I saw. There was something in that small, barely noticeable line that made me feel... real. So I raised the hanger over my head and brought it down onto my leg a little harder, then again and again. It didn't hurt; I don't think I would have continued if it had hurt. It was the mark it left on my skin that made me begin to desire it. I dried myself off and, covered only with a towel, rushed into my parents' room. I hurriedly looked through my dad's things and found his collection of belts. I searched for the one with the biggest buckle on it and excitedly took it to my bedroom. I closed the door and put my nightdress on. Then I took the belt and looked at it: the buckle was the size of my palm and the pin was sharp. I wrapped the belt around my hand twice and whipped my leg with it. This left a much bigger mark than the coat-hanger had. The mark also stayed for longer: it was a good two or three minutes before it faded away. I repeatedly whipped myself with the belt all over my body, on my legs, arms, back and stomach. It didn't feel as though I was trying to punish myself for anything. I didn't feel upset or angry. I felt nothing. While I was whipping myself, all I thought about was what I was doing, and there was no guilt or blame, no emotion at all. It was all so matter-of-fact.

I decided I'd done enough when the pin of the buckle scratched me. It was a tiny scratch, but it hurt and I didn't want to feel pain, so I stopped. I put the belt back in my dad's wardrobe and went to bed.

I didn't know it, but that night everything had changed.

It's surprising how quickly things can become a habit. The following day, while I was at school, I had the urge to hurt myself again. I still hadn't considered this a strange desire, nor thought that something might be wrong; I was completely blank to it. But I asked my English teacher if I could go to the toilet, then went into a cubicle and slapped myself in the face a couple of times. I returned to the classroom feeling calmer and more in control. That evening I stole my dad's belt again and repeated the actions of the night before.

By the third day, hitting myself no longer felt like enough. I sat in my afternoon maths class feeling agitated because I wanted to hurt myself, but I'd tried the slapping actions in the toilets during the morning and that feeling of quietness had not come. We were learning about *pi* and how to work out circumferences at the time, so I was using a compass. I held the purple compass in my right hand and started idly stroking my left hand with its point. I wasn't pushing down hard enough to harm myself – in all the years I've hurt myself, the idea of doing it in front of anyone has always seemed bizarre to me. But this did give me the idea of using the compass. So that night, after I'd said goodnight to my parents, I went upstairs and took the compass out of my Tigger pencil case, got into bed and dragged it across my left arm.

My arm didn't bleed, but the compass did break the skin. The sensation it caused is hard to explain: sedation is probably the best word. I wouldn't say I thought of myself as tense before I used the compass, but the action was still intended to produce a type of serenity. Many doctors and psychiatrists argue that physical pain or the release of blood can cause one's body to produce endorphins, the brain's built-in painkillers, which can provide comfort. Endorphins have a calming effect, but they can also be addictive. I ran the compass across my arm so many times that night that when I eventually switched off the light and went to sleep my whole arm was red.

The next day, when I awoke, I looked at my arm and discovered the scratches hadn't faded. So instead of going downstairs to watch Saturday morning TV in my short-sleeved nightdress as I usually did at the weekend, I showered and dressed so that my parents wouldn't see what I had done. I sat in the house most of the day trying not to think about the marks on my arm. It was the first time since it had begun that I started to think it was a strange thing to do. I'd never heard of the term self-harm before. It wasn't discussed as openly as it is nowadays and so I didn't even know it existed. When my parents suggested that we all go out together to the pub for lunch, I feigned feeling ill so I wouldn't have to join them, and encouraged them to go without me.

Once they were out of the house I went on the internet and typed the words 'deliberate', 'hurting' and 'myself' into a search engine to see if there was any information about it. I was terrified there was going to be nothing, that no one did it or wrote about it, that I was all alone. But what I discovered was that there were many people doing things similar to what I was doing, and that it was called 'self-injury' or 'self-harm'. As I didn't have much time, I skimmed the web pages, looking at the different types of self-injury. But I was worried I might get caught, so I shut down the computer and went upstairs to check my arm. The red lines were still there. It panicked me that they hadn't faded like the coat-hanger and belt marks had. I ran cold water over them to see if it would calm the redness down, but to no avail. As I was trying this, I heard my family come home from the pub, so I pulled the sleeve over my arm and went downstairs to welcome them back. I soon forgot about what I'd done.

That evening I went out with some friends to a quiz night. Will, a boy in the school year above me, was raising money to go on a mission after his GCSEs and the quiz night was in aid of that. I sat with some older friends, one of whom was a 23-year-old man called Chris whom I'd met through a friend of mine he was dating. He had been lodging with Will's family, so came to the quiz night to show his support. He also happened to be a teacher at my school, although he didn't teach me. It was always strange bumping into him at school, as he'd smile and say, 'Hello, Sophie,' and I'd have to reply, 'Hello, Mr Bridges,' which I never really got used to. That evening Chris and I happened to be sitting next to each other while our table tried hopelessly to answer questions. The venue was packed. It was really encouraging to see so many people supporting Will, but it also made the atmosphere very humid. Without thinking, I took my jumper off, revealing the short-sleeved top I was wearing underneath. Chris stared at my arm.

'What on earth happened to you?' he asked.

Anxiously, I tried to think as quickly as possible of a plausible excuse, and for some reason I replied, 'Oh, I fell into a bramble pit!' and laughed to try to make it sound light-hearted.

'It looks really painful. I know brambles scratch you up, but that's ridiculous!' Chris remarked. I agreed with him, giggled almost apologetically and changed the subject back to the quiz.

For the rest of the evening I felt guilty. I'd never been much of a liar; even little fibs always made me feel dire. Consequently this episode made me feel really dreadful. So when I got home, once I'd told my parents about my evening, I went up to my room and added more marks to my arm with the compass. Hurting myself took away that feeling of guilt. It took away every feeling.

When I got into bed that night, the magnitude of the situation started to sink in. I realized something was wrong; that what I was doing wasn't right and I needed to stop it. It was only then that I even considered talking to God about it. That's the strange thing: I had been a committed Christian for three years when I first started self-harming. Did that mean I wasn't actually saved? No. Did it mean I wasn't a 'good' Christian? Definitely, but then who is?

I lay in bed with my earphones in, listening to a worship tape, and cried. I was frightened, really frightened. I didn't know what I was doing or why. I was never a very self-aware person: discovering myself was never an activity that preyed on my mind, which meant all of this was new to me. That made it even scarier. I cried out silently to God for help and felt comforted. For that night, God gave me the same sense of peace that I'd craved when I hurt myself. I also felt him telling me that I needed to speak to Ruth, the youth worker at my church, the next day about what I'd done. He wanted me to give her my compass.

The next day was Sunday. It was fairly easy not to think about the previous night because I was very active all day in my church, St Paul's. I helped with the crèche during the morning service and sang in the band in the evening, starting rehearsals two hours before the service began. This meant I only spent three hours at home: from one o'clock till four. Straight after the evening service we had our youth club, which was one of my favourite times of the week.

I loved going to Space. I had some true friends there who were also Christians. The group had about thirty members, with six youth leaders. It was such a support, great fun, and I think all the young people felt very cared for by the leaders. Every week, we'd meet in the main hall to play very silly, hectic games where the rules always seemed to be seen as 'optional'. We'd then go into another building away from the church, called the Cedar Hall, where there were lots of comfy, albeit very old and dusty, sofas. Here we would have a talk, usually provided by Ruth. I cannot remember what Ruth was talking about that Sunday. I didn't pay much attention because my mind was running through what I was going to tell her afterwards. I think I practised every possible scenario of what could happen, from one of us suddenly dropping dead to the rapture! I was really nervous. I knew Ruth fairly well and she wasn't someone who'd be shocked easily, yet I was still worried she'd be disgusted with me and possibly even reject me entirely. After the talk, we'd split into groups to pray and then go back to the main hall and have fizzy drinks and junk food. Ruth would always stay behind to tidy up after her talk, so I knew I could catch her then and we'd be alone.

As everyone else went across to the main hall, I dawdled, then took a deep breath. I felt as though I was going to faint. I thought to myself, 'Just say it: you need to, and the longer you stay silent like this the harder it'll be.' So, as calmly as possible, I said:

'Ruth, could I have a word?' My heart was racing by now.

'Sure, Sophs, what's up?' Ruth replied casually. She didn't look at me, but just continued picking up the pieces of paper she'd distributed as handouts. We'd never really had a 'Deep and Meaningful Conversation' before, so I doubt she thought the 'word' I wanted was any more than asking her if she'd seen *Neighbours*.

'I need to give you this,' I said, holding out the compass I'd had in my pocket the entire day.

'Riiiight...?' Ruth stopped what she was doing and took the compass from my hand with a confused, slightly concerned look on her face. I froze. I couldn't bring myself to say the words. For all the different scenarios I'd practised, and despite the number of times I'd gone through word for word what I was going to say, when push came to shove I couldn't do it. The awkward silence was thick, and I found it hard to breathe. 'Why have you given me this?' Ruth asked, sensing that I wasn't going to give up the information voluntarily. However, I still couldn't speak. Instead I pulled up my sleeve slightly so she could see a few of the marks on my lower arm.

'Ah,' she sighed, 'let's sit down, shall we?'

HOW GOD MET ME

I became a Christian when I was eight years old. My parents aren't Christians, although they used to say they believed in Christian values and teachings. They had me christened when I was four because they didn't think I would be allowed to go to a Church of England school unless I was. They also used to send me and my brother to our local church, St Paul's, every Sunday morning for Sunday School, while they went home again. I think they saw it as a great babysitting service, as it meant they could have a lie-in without being disturbed by my brother and me watching cartoons all morning.

I don't remember much about Sunday School, but I do remember thinking that all the leaders were really friendly. However, because I didn't have a Christian family, I didn't seem to have the background knowledge which they assumed I had. When we sang the words 'Sing Hosanna to the King' I used to believe that there was a very large female opera singer who was called Hosanna, and we were telling her to sing to the King of Kings. I was genuinely excited that one day we might get to meet Hosanna. I grew up with some knowledge about God and the Bible and believed that he existed, although it was a slightly distorted view.

It was when I was eight that St Paul's decided to hold their first holiday club. Again, my parents thought this was a good idea because it kept me out of trouble for a week in the summer holidays. I loved it. The theme for the week was a press office, and all the children were journalists. We were supposed to interview different members of the Bible about Jesus, then each group would go into their offices – which in reality were giant cardboard boxes placed around the hall, large enough for eight children and two leaders to sit in. Then we'd discuss what we'd found out. I found it really exciting. There were around 100 children and forty leaders in the main hall throughout the week, and to me it was magical.

On the last day of the holiday club, one of the leaders stood up and explained that if we wanted to become friends with Jesus all we had to do was admit we'd done bad things, say sorry, and ask him to be our friend. He then told us all to close our eyes, and said that if anyone wanted to become friends with Jesus they should raise their hand. So I did. I'd always believed that God existed, and the idea of being friends with him seemed brilliant to me. The leader said if those of us who raised our hands wanted to go out and speak to a leader in the Cedar Hall, we could do it now. I got up and went across to the Cedar Hall with twenty other children. I remember there were twenty-one of us because the organizers hadn't expected such a large response and had provided exactly twenty leaders. This meant that as I was the last into the hall, I was paired with another girl to be prayed for. But I didn't mind sharing this special time with someone else.

I was quite a shy child. I didn't seem to acknowledge that timidity in myself, but that's what most adults used to say to me. When I left primary school, my first-year teacher wrote in my leavers' book, 'When you first came here you were so small and quiet. Not so small now, are you?!' So in a way it helped that there was another girl giving her life to God alongside me, because I didn't like too much attention from grown-ups. After I had been prayed for, I realized God was with me. I felt able to chat to him about anything I wanted to, knowing that he'd listen, and I would often feel him replying. This relationship with God carried on until the last year of primary school, when I was ten.

In our school Year 6 we had our second bout of sex education. One lunchtime my friend Rachel and I were sitting on the school field talking about it with a boy called Daniel. He was what all the children in the school affectionately called a MAW boy. MAW stood for Missionaries Across the World, an organization which had its headquarters in the town where I grew up. Missionaries would come and live at the MAW base to train for their missions, and their children would come to my school on the 'MAW bus' every day. Rachel and I asked Daniel if he believed in sex before marriage and he said no. Both of us were shocked and couldn't understand why he said that. He clarified his answer, saying, 'Christians don't believe in sex before marriage.'

I know it's a strange reason to lose one's faith, but this really threw me. My friends and I used to spend every single lunch break reading the problem pages of girls' magazines. We'd giggle about boyfriends and sex all the time, so even though I was only ten and the idea of sex was still a far-off possibility, I didn't want to go against my friends and say I didn't agree with sex before marriage. It was also around this time that my parents told me I didn't have to go to Sunday School any more if I didn't want to. They offered this because they no longer needed anyone to babysit me on Sunday mornings if they wanted a lie-in. I'd stopped enjoying Sunday School, as I was getting too old for it, and this, combined with what had happened at school, meant that I stopped going to church and gradually stopped praying.

In Year 7, when I was twelve, everyone had to move to the much larger and more intimidating secondary schools. Because of the way our county education system worked, people were put in schools according to academic ability. There was a choice of twelve different schools in the area, which meant all friendship groups made in primary schools were broken. I ended up going into a class where I did not know anyone at all.

It was only at my secondary school that I began to realize I was introverted. I had lived in the same house in the same area for my entire life. All my friends at primary school were children I had known at nursery school too. The idea of having to make friends from scratch was new to me. It wasn't something I knew how to do. I wouldn't really talk to anyone, and whenever someone tried to talk to me I'd either be too scared to talk or try too hard to make friends and end up looking silly and scaring them away. After a while it felt as though everyone else in my class had made their friends and I was still by myself. I dreaded lunchtimes and PE lessons in which we were asked to get into pairs – I never had anyone to be my partner. Many people in this situation immerse themselves in work, but I didn't. I didn't work at all. Instead I lay awake all night worrying about the teachers telling me off because of my lack of work.

I did make my one friend, Davina, who was a bully. She was obviously hurting, because she was always trying to get attention. Apart from picking on people and making fun of anyone she could, she would also occasionally bring a handful of paracetamols and a cola bottle filled with Baileys into school. She would then take them in front of everyone, or cut her wrists superficially and then show them to people the next day, telling them she'd tried to kill herself. I watched her doing these things and I think they probably influenced me. Davina was also very sly in her treatment of me, because she knew I was just glad I had a friend. She was very manipulative: if I chatted to anyone else, Davina would sulk, telling me that I obviously couldn't be her best friend if I wanted to chat to 'her'. This meant there was no chance I could make any other friends. Although I had Davina, the times when she would ignore me for weeks on end meant I felt even more alone.

I asked my parents if I could move schools and go to the one that Rachel, my best friend from primary school, went to. They knew I wasn't happy at my school, but they thought it was more academic than the others, and since I hadn't told them how bad it was they said no. I was ashamed to tell my parents that I didn't have any friends and was really unhappy. When no one seemed to want to talk to me, I thought it must be because there was something wrong with me.

Because of the people I was hanging around with, most of the teachers at my school saw me as rebellious and a bully. I spent a lot of my time being told off for not doing my homework, or being shouted at because once again Davina had made someone cry and I was with her. However, one teacher, my form tutor, saw through that and was worried about me. At one point she invited me to come to her room at break time for a chat, but I didn't really understand why she wanted to talk to me. I didn't really trust her, because she was a teacher. She was so worried that she phoned my parents to ask them if there were problems at home, but my parents knew nothing about how I was behaving at school and so they simply said, 'No. Why are you asking?' and my teacher then had to explain everything. When I got home my parents sat me down and gave me a sympathetic lecture about how I should tell them things and not keep secrets. However, I only wanted to protect them from seeing what I saw in myself – worthlessness.

I was finding it increasingly hard to sleep, because I worried about school, teachers, homework and lack of friends. I was tired all the time and so I started praying again, at first just asking God if he'd help me to sleep. This never worked, however. I now realize it was because God wanted me to face my problems and also come closer to him. But at the time I started to resent God because he wouldn't do this one thing I asked of him. So things continued to get worse. At lunchtimes at school I used to sit in a little hidden spot under the stairs so no one would see me – and no one would know what a loser I was. Teachers got even more infuriated with me, and I started talking back to them because I'd heard it all before. My form tutor really tried to help me but whenever she tried to speak to me I would become self-defending and nothing good ever came from it.

I got so tired of everything that my bedtime prayer to God changed from asking him to let me sleep to asking that he'd let me sleep – and never wake me up. That was how I'd pray it. I didn't want to feel ashamed of not having friends or to be told off for not working, I was upset for upsetting my parents, and I was just so tired. Every morning when I woke up I became more bitter towards God because I thought either he just didn't exist or he did exist and wouldn't answer my prayer because he wanted me to suffer. After a few months I gave up praying and decided that if God wasn't going to help me, I'd have to do it myself.

I didn't see myself as 'suicidal', because after being friends with Davina I thought everyone was doing it. When my parents went out one evening I went to the medicine cupboard and took five paracetamols and went to bed. I realize now that that isn't even close to enough for an overdose, but I didn't know how many I really needed to take at the time. Thankfully, I woke up. But I awoke even more miserable, because I couldn't even kill myself properly. A couple of weeks later I decided to do something that wouldn't fail. I sneaked out of the house at ten o'clock and walked to the nearest railway bridge.

I stood on the bridge, looking down at the track for a long time. It was a cold night and the wind blew straight through me, making me shiver. Every time a car went past I pretended to be just walking along the bridge, in case they worried about me. While I was waiting for a train to come a thought kept going through my mind: 'This can't be it. There must be something more to life than this. You can't just be born, suffer and die – there must be something more than this.' At the time, I thought it was just me being scared and a wimp, so I kept trying to fight it. Now I know it was God, and he was determined to keep that thought going through my head. I stood there for about thirty minutes, and although it was a busy railway line, no train came. Because of that and the thought going around my head, I gave up and went home again. I walked home cursing myself for being too scared and cursing the railway company for not having enough trains!

After this incident I felt terrible and cross with myself, as I still thought I was just being scared. But then a week later one of my old friends, with whom I'd lost contact since changing schools, invited me to go on a weekend away with her church, St Paul's. I was cross with her for calling it her church when I still saw it as just as much mine as hers, even though I hadn't been in a couple of years. But I was also really pleased she'd invited me, and decided to go. I still considered myself a Christian, even though by this point I hated God. I thought the weekend would be just a nice, fun time and that afterwards I'd go back to the bridge and get the job done properly.

About thirty young people went on the weekend. It was fun. We played lots of silly games, such as how many things beginning with P can you fit into a matchbox, and wide games involving running around trying to steal flags. On the Saturday night we all met together to listen to a talk by the leader. To be honest, I cannot remember what he talked about. All I can remember is a song that the worship leader sang, called 'What a Friend I've Found'. The words were:

What a friend I've found
Closer than a brother
I have felt your touch
More intimate than lovers

Jesus, Jesus
Jesus
Friend for ever

Martin Smith © 1996 Curious? Music, UK

I stood there listening to the words being played over and over, and the thought started going through my head again: 'There has to be more to life than this.' I wondered whether what was being sung could be true – even for me. I'd convinced myself that God wouldn't want me because I was so worthless and bad, that his not answering my prayer to let me die somehow proved he didn't care. Jesus might want to be other people's friend, but not mine.

When the song finished, the musicians kept playing the melody while the leader stood up and asked anyone who wanted to become a Christian to go to the front to be prayed for. I found the idea of going to the front really frightening. However, as I was convinced that I was a Christian already, I comforted myself that I was fine and didn't need to go. But after a few minutes the leader stood up again and said:

'Right... this is a little unusual, but if there's anyone here who is a Christian but wants to make their peace with God, would you like to come up to be prayed for?'

I thought, 'Oh no! Please don't let that be me!' I looked around to see if anyone else was going up, but no one did. The longer I waited, the more sure I was that God was asking me to go and be prayed for.

Eventually I left my seat and speed-walked to the front, hoping that no one would see me going. I tried to hide myself among the others so that none of the leaders would be able to see me, or even get close to me to offer prayer, but someone did. I had my eyes closed, partly because I was praying to God, but mainly because of the childish belief that if we close our eyes no one can see us. One of the men put his hand on my shoulder and asked if I was OK. I'd never been in this position before and I had no idea what I was supposed to do or say – so I didn't say anything; I just kept my eyes shut tight and nodded. He started praying for me, while I just listened to the melody of the song and sang it in my head.

Suddenly it all clicked into place. God didn't want me to die, not because he wanted me to suffer but because I was his friend and he loved me too much and had too many plans for me to allow that to happen. It didn't matter that I didn't have any friends, because I had the best friend in the world. When the man praying for me asked for the Holy Spirit to come into my life, I actually wanted him to. I really felt him come. He didn't make me shake or cry or laugh, and I think that's because that would have been too much for me to take at that time, as I still found it hard to trust people – even God. Instead he came very gently but let me know he was there. I felt the pain inside me, that I'd been trying to ignore, lift.

That was a few years before the harming began. Since then, things had been getting gradually better. Because I knew God was with me, it gave me some self-confidence that enabled me to stand up to people, even Davina, when I felt I was being used. This lack of need for friendships, ironically, meant that I started to gain more friends. I started to do my homework and stopped talking back to my teachers. I even discovered that my form teacher who'd been trying to help me was a Christian. I felt more of a bond with her and was more willing to allow her to help me.

By the time I was fifteen I'd been going to church every week and built up a set of close friends there. I had joined the youth group and the Bible study group. It was through these groups that I met Ruth.

'How long has this been going on?' Ruth asked, looking at me. I rapidly realized that this thing I'd been doing to myself was no longer something only I knew about. I hadn't thought of it as a secret before, but now I wished it was. I was ashamed.

'Just under a week. It's no big deal really,' I back-pedalled.

'OK, well you need to stop this now,' Ruth replied, still sounding caring, but with a sense of urgency in her voice. 'If you don't, it can become a habit that you'll find hard to break.'

I couldn't understand that. I still wasn't that aware of what self-harm was, so the idea that someone could get addicted to hurting themselves didn't make any sense to me.

'Why did you do it?' she asked.

'I don't know,' I replied honestly. 'I just sort of... started.' I explained to her the incident with the coat-hanger and how it had progressed to what I'd shown her. I felt some comfort in the fact that she didn't seem disgusted or even shocked by what I was telling her. But a small part of me kept telling myself that she was covering the disgust and she actually thought I was a freak.

Ruth asked me if we could pray about it and I agreed. She said a prayer for me, thanking God that I'd been brave and told her what I'd done and asking him to help me not to do it again. The problem was I didn't think I had a problem. I couldn't believe it could become a habit, and still less could I believe that I could get into the habit and struggle to get out again. So I didn't really pray the prayer with her. I thanked Ruth for her help and we walked back to the main hall together. As we walked, Ruth said that she was going to ask me again at some point how it was going – that she wasn't going to let this rest. I said OK, but inside I was just thinking, 'It's fine, it's not that big a deal. I don't need to do this, I just sometimes want to.'

Consequently, when I got home from Space that night I didn't hurt myself. In fact, I didn't do anything for two days, until I was given the present of a compass by a friend because I'd 'lost' mine and still needed one for maths.

3.

IT CONTINUES

Maybe if I hadn't needed a compass for maths at the time I could have stopped and never looked back, but I doubt it. I took the new, pretty pink compass up to my room that night and ran it over my skin again. But this time I felt nothing. This time I wanted to do more; this time I needed to see blood. The compass wasn't very sharp, so although it broke the skin, even when I pressed down really hard it didn't seem to bleed. After using the compass for an hour I started to get frustrated. I sneaked downstairs, past the living room where my parents were watching TV, and took a knife out of a drawer in the kitchen. I put it under my jumper and went back up to my room. I ran this over my arm, thinking it would cut me, but it didn't do a thing. It didn't even leave a red mark, let alone break the skin. So I picked up my compass again and decided to run it over the same area repeatedly to see if that would work. It did. A small, red bead appeared on my skin. The sight of blood actually excited me a little: I felt a sense of achievement because of the length of time it took to get it. I wiped the bead away with a tissue and saw the small hole in my skin from where it had come. I put the compass in the gap and pulled at the edge of the hole, creating a longer scratch. It still wasn't deep, but it created a few small, separate scarlet beads on my skin. I cannot really explain what was going through my head at the time, except thoughts about how to make my arm bleed more. I was not thinking about any situation or feeling any emotion. I was solely concentrating on what I was doing, and that gave me a sense of control and calmed me.

After a while the tissue I was using to wipe the blood started to look quite spotty, covered in many small red dots. I liked this: I felt a sense of pride in the amount I had managed to bleed. However, what Ruth had said about checking up on me still rang in my ears. Although I wanted to continue making the tissue redder, I decided that I wouldn't cut or scratch my arms in any place except in that one point that I'd already made bleed. I somehow sincerely thought that this was better and more acceptable. This is what I continued to do daily, each time making the singular scratch more into a cut, longer, wider and deeper.

The next Sunday at Space, Ruth was true to her word and asked me how everything was going, and I said OK. She didn't seem convinced, and asked,

'Are you sure?'

I said, 'Yes, I'm not doing it like I was before. I'm only doing one cut – it's not covering my whole arm, it's fine.'

Ruth looked sceptical and slowly said, 'Ye-e-e-s...'

When Ruth led Bible studies with my youth group, if someone answered one of the questions incorrectly, instead of saying, 'No, you're wrong,' she'd reply, 'Ye-e-e-s...' to try to encourage us. Everyone in the group knew this meant no; it just sounded friendlier. This was the response that I received from her now.

'Really, it's fine!' I tried to assure her.

'Well, if you think it is, I'll leave it for now; but I will be keeping an eye on you.'

'I really am fine, it's fine.' I felt the need to repeat myself again and again, probably more to reassure myself than Ruth. Part of me knew it wasn't OK, but I didn't want to stop.

Over the next few weeks the self-harm began to get worse. I wasn't happy unless I'd made the cut on my arm bleed at least once a day. During school hours, if I went to the toilet, I would pick at the scab in order to open up the wound and then when I was at home I'd use my compass again. This continued until one day, while I was in the house alone, I knocked over a glass of lemonade I'd been drinking and it smashed into hundreds of pieces. It was one of my mum's favourite glasses, and I was so cross with myself that without thinking I picked up one of the pieces of shattered glass and passed it across my arm. The glass was so sharp that it glided across my skin easily and caused many small red droplets to appear immediately. It thrilled me to see how effortless it was compared to the other cut, which was hard work with my compass. This might sound stupid, but apart from knives, over the couple of months since I'd started self-harming I'd never thought of any other apparatus that would work better than my humble compass. But now, the broken glass excited me because it was so simple and swift. I ran it over my arm repeatedly, completely dismissing the rule that I'd promised to Ruth about only making one cut. I needed to do this, I told myself at the time: I'd just lie to her if she asked again.

After that I used broken glass every time. I also joined a support group on the internet, where people talked about what they did and what they used. It was supposed to be a group in which people encouraged each other to stop. But in fact it was a very negative place, where people seemed to feel the need to compete with each other for the worst injuries. It was here that I heard all sorts of stories and gained lots of tips on how to hurt myself more effectively (this website has now closed down). In a very short time I learnt that razor blades were the best thing to use, so one Saturday afternoon, while my family were at a garden centre, I took one of my dad's disposable razors and used a biro to prise the safety clasp off the blade.

Razors became my instrument of choice from then on. However, I also started doing other things. I would punch or kick walls, or hit myself in the face. A few times I went into the tool shed beside my house, picked up a sledgehammer and battered my foot with it. All these things I would do for the same reason: that sense of release and calmness. I never felt any pain.

While harming myself I wouldn't think of anything except what I was doing.

One day, about four months later, I went into the tool shed to use the sledgehammer on my foot again. It gave me the usual sense of relief and release, but after a few seconds I started to feel the throbbing pain. It hurt, it really hurt. I wasn't used to pain, as that was never my intention. I looked down at my foot and I could see it had already started swelling. I panicked that I might have broken a bone. I didn't know what to do, so I wrapped it tightly in a bandage and prayed that it would be OK. I felt guilty praying that God would help me with something that I'd inflicted on myself.

Usually, when I hurt myself I would ignore God and pretend to myself either that he didn't exist or that somehow he wasn't watching. I knew I was sinning, but didn't want to stop. This was the only way I could continue doing what I was doing. I felt the same as a small child who'd close her eyes, stick her fingers in her ears and sing 'La la la,' pretending that if she couldn't hear or see, it couldn't be real. It felt as though if I didn't feel or acknowledge God, then I couldn't disappoint or upset him.

That evening, while I was preparing my family's dinner, my mum asked me:

'Dear me, Sophs, what have you done to your foot?'

'Oh, I fell off the front step,' I giggled. I'd been planning the lie since I put the bandage on.

'My gosh, you are in the wars nowadays, aren't

you? If it's not that it's something else! Is it OK? It's really swollen.'

'Yeah, it's fine, just a bit bruised.' I shrugged it off and went back to cooking. When my mum left the room, however, I paused and repented to God for having to lie yet again.

Two days later I helped lead worship in a youth service at church, singing in the band. I still needed to wear the bandage on my foot, and so a few people at the rehearsal asked me what had happened. Every time I lied. Ruth didn't ask. During the service, while I was singing at the front and praising God, I felt God really convict me about the self-harm. I didn't want to tell Ruth that I was hurting myself a lot more than before, because I was worried that she'd be disappointed in me, so I decided to speak to the curate, Brian, who was leading the service.

I was often one of the last people to leave church after the youth service, so it wasn't unusual for Brian and me to be the last ones packing up. We chatted as we were both tidying and I brought up the topic of flagellation, just as a way to introduce self-harm. For years I couldn't say the words self-harm or injury, cut, hurt, or any other words to do with self-harm at all, because I was so ashamed of it. Instead I managed to say that the bandage on my foot wasn't entirely an accident. Brian stopped what he was doing and looked at me. He asked:

'Is that what you think you're doing – flagellation?'

I said that if I was honest, no. I'd just wanted to

discern his opinion about any form of hurting oneself. He asked me why I did it, and that question seemed to open up some floodgates.

'I don't know why I do it. I can't stop. I know it's horrible and disgusting and that God doesn't want me to do it but I still do. I can't not do it. I just pretend God's not there. I avoid him when I want to do this. It's happening every day, if not more than that, and in some ways I don't want to stop, but I want to want to stop. I really felt challenged by God about it tonight – that it hurts him when do I this stuff. But I still don't think I can stop it.

'I hate it. I hate the lies too. I hate lying to people if they see a mark I didn't hide fast enough. I hate hiding from my parents. Now when I go for a shower, I take my clothes into the bathroom too, because I can't pop across from my bedroom to the bathroom in just my towel in case my parents happen to see my arms. I hate telling everyone that I slipped off a step when they ask why I have this bandage on my ankle.

'I hate all of this, it's horrible. But I can't stop it.'

By this point I was almost in tears. I didn't like crying in front of people, so I looked away and took a few deep breaths. When I looked back Brian was still just looking at me, with an expression on his face I couldn't read.

'What?' I asked him. I'd always worry when I didn't know what people were thinking.

'I'm just thinking... that must make you feel so... s**t,' he replied.

I'd known Brian for a couple of years and had never heard him swear. He wasn't the type of person who normally would, and so this came as a real shock to me. Yet somehow that word seemed entirely appropriate and necessary at that moment. It encapsulated how I felt about myself and my self-harm.

'Yes,' I agreed, and burst into tears.

Brian let me cry for a while, and then very calmly asked me:

'Shall we pray about it?'

'OK,' I sniffed, and we sat down to pray. Brian prayed out loud and I prayed in my head. I wasn't ready to stop self-harming, but we prayed that I'd want to want to stop, which made more sense to me. I felt God telling me that he wasn't going to leave me on this, that he was involved and I wasn't alone, even when I did it, which I found both convicting and comforting – as only God can do.

I went home that night and was so tired that I went straight to bed.

Although I now knew God was with me even when I was pretending he wasn't, I still wanted to hurt myself, and did so the next day. That evening Ruth phoned me and asked if I could come to the church because she and Brian needed to chat with me. I said OK, and that I'd see her on Wednesday after school.

I didn't know what she wanted to talk to me about. I thought it must be serious because she'd never asked me to do that before. I worried it might have been about the self-harm. But then it could have been to do with the youth service I was heavily involved with, or to ask me to help with another project, or to discuss an issue about someone else in the youth group.

On Wednesday I got off the school bus four stops earlier than usual and walked to church. As I walked I prayed that whatever it was they wanted to talk to me about, God would be there and in control and his will would be done. I went to the church office and found Ruth practising on the piano.

'Hey, Sophs!' she exclaimed, sounding a little too excited, which told me she was nervous. 'Brian isn't here yet, as usual, so we'll have to wait a while. How was school?'

We chatted until Brian turned up and then Ruth and Brian led me into a smaller room with three chairs already set up. As soon as I saw this, and realized there'd been preparation involved, I knew it was about my self-harm.

We sat down and Ruth began:

'Sophie, I know you told Brian that your self-injury is still continuing, and not just that, but that it's getting worse. Is that right?'

'Yes,' I replied, not knowing where this conversation was going to lead.

'Well, the law says that if you're under sixteen and you're at risk to yourself or to others, we have to tell your parents.'

My heart didn't so much miss a beat as feel as though it had jumped into my throat.

'I'm not at risk to myself!' I argued.

'You're hurting yourself, Sophie – that's risk,' Ruth replied calmly.

'But I'm going to be sixteen in three months. Please don't tell my parents,' I begged.

'We don't want to have to,' Ruth replied. 'That's why Brian and I have brought you here. We think it'd be better if you told them instead.'

'I can't!' I began to cry. 'Seriously, I can't. It's just not possible.'

'If you don't then we'll have to,' said Ruth.

'Please,' I begged, tears rolling down my cheeks.

'It's not our decision any more, Sophie,' Brian stepped in. 'We're here because we care about you, but it's the law and there's nothing more we can do about it. But what we thought was that while we're here you can practise – imagine Ruth and I are your parents and tell us.'

'I can't believe this,' I said. I really couldn't. I couldn't have imagined in a million years that this would happen when I met up with Ruth and Brian. I sat there in the silence, thinking that somehow this wasn't real and that I wasn't sitting there with them. I just didn't want to believe it.

'Do you want to try telling us?' Ruth asked sensitively.

'I just can't.'

'Try.' Now it felt real.

'Please, just pretend I didn't tell you.'

'You know we can't do that, Sophie.' Brian replied. 'It doesn't work that way.'

'And we wouldn't want to do that – to you or ourselves,' Ruth added.

'So this is really the only way?' I asked, pleading with them to find another option.

'It is,' Ruth answered.

'I really think this is for the best too, Sophs,' Brian said. 'I mean, remember you said you hated hiding your arms from your parents? Come on, try pretending we're your parents and tell us.'

I thought about this. I still couldn't believe I was going to have to tell my parents that I'd been hurting myself. Yet I thought Brian was right, that practising it first was a good idea. So I tried.

'OK... I guess at first I'd have to wait until Dad came home from work and then tell them I needed to speak to them about something.'

'Good,' Ruth encouraged.

'So I'd ask them to sit down and then I'd say...' I couldn't do it. 'Then I'd say, "I..."' I paused again. 'I can't do this!' I gave up. 'This is crazy. I can't even tell you two and you know what I'm doing! How on earth am I supposed to tell my parents? Please don't make me do this, please.'

'Sophie...'

'I can't do this. I can't say the words. I've never been able to say the words out loud – and now I've got to say them out loud for the first time in front of my parents? It's impossible!'

'You have to. If you don't, we'll have to tell them, and I think it'd be so much better if it came from you,' Ruth said firmly.

Eventually, after two hours of trying to negotiate, I realized that the choice was out of their hands. I wouldn't be able to convince them not to make me. So I said OK, and that I'd tell my parents that evening when my dad got back from work.

Ruth and Brian told me they'd be praying for me and would ask me how it went.

That evening when I got home I asked my mum when Dad would get back.

'Well, he's got a work do on tonight, so not till around ten o'clock, maybe,' she replied.

'Oh, OK,' I said, 'I kinda need to speak to you two about something when he gets back.'

'OK, Sophs, but I'm not sure what time he'll be back: it could be late.'

'That's OK,' I replied, and hurried up to my bedroom.

At about ten o'clock, just as Mum had said, I heard my dad coming through the door. I was starting to get nervous, so I crept out of my room, sat on the stairs and listened to my parents talking in the kitchen.

'Sophs wants a chat with us,' Mum said.

'Oh really, what about?'

'I have no idea, but it sounds quite serious – she's asked to speak to both of us.'

'Right then, I'll go and tell her I'm home,' Dad replied.

With that I jumped up and started casually walking down the stairs, pretending I hadn't been listening.

'Hey Dad,' I said, acting as nonchalant as possible.

'Hello, sweetheart, I hear you want to talk to us.'

'Yeah... er... could we go into the living room?'

I stood at the door while my parents settled down on the sofa. I felt sick. I didn't want to tell them. I didn't want my parents to be disappointed in me, or upset or angry. I had no idea how they were going to react, but I couldn't think of any response that would be good. My heart was pounding and I felt dizzy, so I leaned against the door frame to steady myself.

'Right, what is it you wanted to tell us, sweetheart?' Mum asked.

'Well...'

'Oh, I know: you want to be a nun!' my dad joked. My parents would sometimes tease me because of my relationship with God. It was only in jest and I think my dad made this very bad joke because he was nervous, as the situation seemed very grave. I had never had to 'sit my parents down' before this night. I think they must have thought I was going to tell them I was pregnant or had been taking drugs. I know they had no idea that I was going to tell them this. However, whatever the reason for my dad making that silly joke, he'd just made the situation a whole lot harder for me.

'No, Dad.' I tried to laugh. 'I, er... I don't know whether you've had any suspicions or anything, but for the past few months...' I took a deep breath, 'I've been hurting myself.' I froze; I couldn't think of anything else to say. My mind went blank.

The silence seemed to go on for ever. My mum was the first person to break it.

'Why don't you come and sit down?' she asked calmly, holding her hand out towards me. I knew she was trying to keep calm for me but I also knew that although she wasn't showing it, I'd really upset her. I couldn't cope with it.

'No. Sorry!' I panicked and ran up to my room, closing the door behind me. I dived under the duvet and cried. I was shaking so much that I had to hold myself to keep myself still. I lay cocooned in my bed in darkness.

That night, all I could hear was my mother crying downstairs.

4.

PRAYERS AND ANSWERS

Throughout my childhood I'd had a fairly close relationship with my parents. I didn't get to see my dad a lot during the week, because his job meant he'd have to live away from home or get home after I'd gone to bed, but he'd make it up to my brother and me at the weekend. We'd go out most weekends to museums or zoos or to the river to feed the swans. When I was about six my brother and I used to fight over who could sit next to him if we went to McDonald's; I guess I was a bit of a daddy's girl. However, because of my dad's absence during the week, I saw my mum as my more stable role model. She was the one who'd come to my ballet shows and drama competitions and who'd tuck me in at night.

My parents rarely fought. In fact I can only remember one time when I saw them having an argument, and that was when I was eight years old. It was early in the morning and I was sitting at the table in the living room, lost in my own little world of Coco Pops, when I noticed that my mum, who was sitting on the sofa, had her head tilted away from me and was covering eyes with her hand. I realize now that my parents must have been bickering for quite a while before this moment, but I was completely oblivious.

'What's wrong, Mummy?' I asked her, quite confused.

'Gosh, now you're going to take her side, aren't you?' my dad retaliated. In my world this came completely out of the blue. It suddenly struck me that my mum was crying and my dad looked frustrated – as if he was no longer in control of the situation. As I'd never seen this before, and I didn't like the way my dad had spoken to me, I started crying as well.

'Argh, now you're crying too!'

Dad threw his hands up in the air in defeat and stormed out of the house.

Both my mum and I sat there in silent sobs for a few seconds, me not knowing what had just happened, and my mum not knowing what to do. Then my mum said, 'Come here, you daft sausage.' She held her arms out to me, and without a moment's hesitation I ran into them.

A few minutes later my dad returned with a bunch of flowers for my mum and a chocolate bar for me, looking fairly sheepish and saying how sorry he was for making the two most important women in his life cry. We all had a kiss and a cuddle and things were fine again.

As I grew up, one reason why my parents and I weren't as close as we could have been was that from a very early age I kept secrets from them. If the school bully at my primary school decided to pick on me for the day, or if I'd grazed my knee and had to see the school nurse, I wouldn't tell my mum when I got home. The secrets varied in size and importance, but it was something that I'd always done and I didn't see as a bad thing. I know that many children keep secrets from their parents, and that it's not unusual. But for me, it meant that keeping my self-harm secret came more naturally.

The morning after telling my parents I'd been cutting myself, I 'accidentally-on-purpose' overslept. I quickly washed and changed in my room, then ran out of the house, shouting 'Bye,' without having to see anyone. At school, I spent the whole day worrying about what was going to happen when I got home. I couldn't work and barely spoke to anyone. I was chewing pen caps so much, I think I must have eaten about three of them that day!

I walked home from school the long way round. When I got home, as casually as possible I dumped my bag in the hallway, slumped on the sofa and switched on the TV. My mum came in and sat down next to me. I took a deep breath, ready for a confrontation about the events of the previous night, but she didn't say a word. Neither my mum nor my dad has ever really mentioned it since then. There have been slight references to it through the years, such as my mum asking me how I got a scar on my arm, but no big discussion. This seems to be the most common reaction when it comes to self-harm.

So life returned to normal, my parents pretending nothing had happened and me continuing to hide my self-harm habit from them. By this point I had a box in which I kept all my injuring tools and aids. Inside was a knife and a biro that I used to break open razors; antiseptic cream which I'd never used but was there just in case a cut became infected; butterfly stitches to hold the cut together if it was wide so it would scar less; plasters and bandages. I kept it covered with bed sheets in a drawer at the bottom of my wardrobe. For a while after I'd told my parents, my self-harm reduced in frequency because I was worried they might come into my room and catch me in the act. But the extent of damage I did in a harming session grew worse. By now both of my arms were lacerated in cuts of different ages, so I had to move on to other places that were also easy to cover up. However, for someone who had to wear a skirt to school and only a long-sleeved leotard to dance lessons this was harder than it might seem. My feet and my stomach became the new canvases for my sad art.

I was the 'smiley, happy, bubbly' girl everywhere I went. I'm unsure how much of that was an act and how much of it was genuinely me being myself. The desire to hurt myself only seemed to happen when I was alone; when I was with friends I felt fine. This often meant I was the last one to leave my youth group on Sundays. I think the leaders used to get really frustrated with this, but it was because part of me simply didn't want to go home. It was the same at parties and gatherings with my friends: I never wanted to leave them. Even if my parents were there, if I was at home I had the opportunity to hurt myself, and so home meant harm.

To keep out of the house, I started going for frequent walks. I'd walk around my home town for literally hours on end. I'd just walk and listen to music on my CD player, trying not to think about wanting to hurt myself. I used to tell my parents, 'I'm going for a walk.' I think they thought I was actually sneaking off to a boyfriend's house, because they'd always let me go even though they knew it would be for a very long time. Sometimes, when I was feeling at my worst, I would go for walks late into the night. I realize that this wasn't the safest thing to do, but my opinion at the time was that there was more of a risk at home than on the streets.

Occasionally I'd walk past St Paul's, sneak into the graveyard through a hole in the fence and sit on a step next to the hut used for crèche on Sunday mornings. I liked sitting there, because there was a hedge in front of the step so no one could see me. I felt completely safe from the world; no one knew about this spot and no one knew I was there. This place became my haven, where I would sit and pray to God whenever I felt down. Sometimes I'd shout at him and blame him for everything that was going wrong in my life, accusing him of not protecting me. Sometimes I'd cry to him about how sorry I was for not following him, and other times I'd just sit there in silence and feel his presence with me.

That's one thing I still find amazing about God: his ability to put up with me. None of this was really God's fault, I knew that then as well as now, and yet I needed to yell and shout and blame someone – and he was there. God knew that I was angry with him, and if I'd pretended I wasn't I'd only have been fooling myself. He wanted me to tell him, so I screamed at him, had a tantrum and shook my fists and stamped my feet until I was too tired to do anything but rest in his unfailing love. God can cope with people being angry with him, even though it isn't his fault – his shoulder is big enough.

After a while I started to worry that I was being a hassle for Ruth and Brian, so I stopped talking to them about my self-harm. I know now that it wasn't true and that they didn't feel annoyed with me or burdened by me. But for some people who have low self-esteem, as I did, fears of being a nuisance are very big. Instead I carried on going to Space and pretending that everything was fine, until one night when I had a fight with a friend of mine.

If I'm honest, I can't even remember what the fight was about. I don't think it was anything that important, but I do remember it being quite dramatic and the whole youth group watching. Ruth wasn't around that night, so some of the volunteers were looking after the group instead. The two in particular who were leading it, a married couple called Bev and Gary, were setting up in the other building.

Once my friend Clare and I had finished screaming at one another, I stormed out. I was crying and didn't like people to see me cry, so I just wanted to be anywhere but there. As I was walking away, some of the girls started following me, begging me to go back. I know that often girls (myself included) storm out of places, wanting their friends to follow, but this time I really didn't want them to. I kept walking and telling them to leave me alone.

'Sophie, come back, please!' Alice said, running to keep up with me.

'Seriously, guys, please, just leave me alone.'

'You can't just walk out,' Suzanne shouted.

'Watch me,' I said, leaving the gates of the church and continuing to walk.

My friends stopped and watched me go, then went back to tell everyone I'd left. I just continued walking. I stormed around, trying to get out of my system the horrible feeling left by my row with Clare. I didn't want to go back home looking as though I'd been crying, so I wandered around the woods near my house for a while.

When I got home I pretended everything was fine in front of my parents. They asked me why I was back so early and I said that I didn't feel too well. I went into my dad's office and logged on to the internet. I spent the next few hours on message boards for self-harmers, chatting to people and venting my feelings about the argument I'd just had. Eventually, my mum came in and told me I needed to go to bed.

The next day at school I discovered how much aggro I had caused the night before. Apparently when I'd walked out, Gary had driven around the whole of my town looking for me. When he'd returned to Space without success, Bev had tried phoning me at home, but by that time I was on the internet so she could not get through. The whole youth club was worried about me, not knowing where I'd gone or if I was safe. This meant most of my friends were quite understandably cross with me. They insisted that that evening I should phone Bev and Gary and let them know what had happened and that I was OK.

I got home from school and decided that if I was going to phone Bev and Gary I'd better do it straight away, otherwise I'd probably panic and back out. Before I fed the cats or even took my shoes off, I searched through old leaflets advertising Space and found their number, went up to my room and dialled.

Bev answered the phone.

'Hi, Bev, it's Sophie here.'

'Oh, hi, Sophie, how are you?

'I'm OK. I just wanted to apologize for walking out of Space last night.'

'It's OK. Is everything all right? What happened?'

I wasn't really sure what to say. Bev knew that everything wasn't all right, otherwise I wouldn't have stormed off the night before. I decided to try to play it cool.

'Oh, it was just a silly fight with Clare. I'm sorry: I shouldn't have left.'

'No, you shouldn't have. Gary and I were really worried about you. But I'm pleased to hear you're OK. Would you like to come round for a cup of tea tomorrow?'

'Er... OK, sure.' I felt quite suspicious of Bev's offer of tea. I wasn't sure why she was asking me but I thought it would be really rude to say no after everything I'd put her through the night before. My school had a teachers' training day the next day, which meant students didn't have to attend, so I arranged to meet Bev after lunch.

Bev was (and still is) a very warm, encouraging and caring person who always saw the best in people, and it didn't take long before she became my mentor and confidante. I felt safe with her, and would often pop round to her house after school and help her with her children. I felt I could tell her everything I was thinking and feeling and that she wouldn't judge me for it. I used to phone her whenever I felt 'triggered' to hurt myself and she'd just listen to me; often a listening ear was all I needed. Sometimes, however, I'd call her but hang up again because I was embarrassed or ashamed, or felt I would be wasting her time and I wasn't worth it.

After a while Bev decided she needed to set some boundaries with me about this. She told me that I was not allowed to phone her and hang up: either I phoned or I didn't, but I mustn't just hang up. I also had a deadline of nine o'clock at night: I could not phone her past this time. When she first told me she'd made these rules I felt really hurt and unwanted, and childishly decided that I'd never phone her again. That didn't last long, however, because the next time I found myself triggered or upset she was the first person I wanted to speak to. I quickly learned that Bev was very wise to set those rules to protect both of us. If she hadn't, our relationship would have become difficult, because she needed something in place to remind her that it was not her fault if I cut myself. She also needed space to spend time with her husband in the evenings, and I needed something in place to stop me becoming too dependent on her.

When we talked, Bev would try to encourage me to throw my razors away, but this was something I found I couldn't do. Instead, I'd seal them in an envelope, take them round to her house and give them to Bev to throw away. I think I found this easier because I didn't have to see them being thrown away. I could somehow convince myself that Bev was just 'holding on to them' for me and I could go back and pick them up again if I really needed to. She would encourage me to read the Bible and pray whenever I felt that I wanted to hurt myself. We'd also pray together most times we met. This became a regular routine for the next few years.

When I was sixteen my self-harm seemed to reach its worst level in terms of frequency. I would cut myself almost every day, and sometimes more than once a day. It seemed to be ruling my life. It felt as though I had no control over it, as though I was simply surviving between each injuring session. Every night, whether I'd hurt myself or not, I would go to bed and put on some Christian music and cry to God. I still knew that he didn't want me to be doing this, and I hated the fact that I was hurting him by hurting myself.

One night when I was in the house by myself, I had put on some Christian music and was just resting in God's presence. As I was listening to the music I heard a voice, not one in my head but a soft, audible male voice. It was a strange moment, because although there was no one but me in the house it didn't scare me at all. I somehow knew it was God. The voice simply said,

'Sophie, I want you to do something for me.'

My immediate reaction was, 'Oh yes, God's calling me to be a great missionary or world speaker! Look out, Samuel, here comes Sophie!' With a lot of excitement I whispered back,

'Yes, God, what is it?'

'Sophie, I want you to say out loud three times, "God, you love me."'

What? How was that going to get me famous? How was that going to cause thousands of people to flock to me asking me how they could repent? At that moment, I thought God's request was pretty stupid. However, I reasoned that maybe God wanted me to say this sentence and then he would tell me what he needed me and only me to do.

'Er, OK.' I took a breath. 'God, you love...' I paused. I couldn't say it. Instead, I decided to try different words:

'God, you love... the world.'

'God, you love... us.'

'God, you love... EVERYONE!'

These sentences came easily, but I knew that that wasn't what God was asking me to say. I sat there for a while, slightly confused that I found such a small word so hard to utter. But I tried again:

'God, you love...' I still couldn't do it. I sat on my bedroom floor, still listening to the music, and started crying. I no longer cared about the great mission I thought God was going to send me on; I just wanted to be able to say those four words.

I prayed to God that he'd show me why I couldn't make myself say a simple sentence that a toddler could articulate. Gradually I realized it was because although I thought I knew that God loved me, I really didn't. I didn't feel that I could be loved by God, because I wasn't worth it. This was what God wanted me to do: not to become a world-famous missionary but to realize that he loved me, me personally.

After about half an hour filled with crying, praying and struggling to appreciate what God was trying to persuade me to do, I managed to say it:

'God, you love me.

'God, you love me.

'God, you love me.'

Once I'd managed to say what God had asked me to, I was filled with a great sense of his peace and joy. I no longer knew what to say to him, but it didn't matter because God gave me a gift of his – speaking in tongues.

So, that was it? After that moment I knew that God loved me and I no longer felt the need to hurt myself? I went on and lived happily ever after? I really wish I could say that, but self-harm rarely works that way. It's self-destructive, and often the better you feel, the more you feel the need to hurt yourself. What changed in that moment, was that I knew God loved me – forget everyone else, he loved me and died for me. If I'd been the only person in the world who ever sinned, he would have still died for me. That is true for you also. This real heart-knowledge meant that I could trust God wouldn't leave me, even when I did things wrong. God is gracious and he loves you and me.

The gift of tongues helped when I was feeling bad. I didn't know why I was feeling the way I was, and I felt lost and confused, so the idea that I could pray to God knowing that I was saying exactly what he wanted me to, even without me knowing it, was really encouraging. Whenever I prayed and felt lost for words I could speak in tongues and be assured that it didn't matter that I didn't know what to say, because God knew anyway. I really thank God for that gift.

One evening when I was seventeen, I felt horribly triggered. I was convinced I was going to hurt myself, but I decided to call Bev instead. We talked for a couple of hours on the phone about how I wanted, yet didn't want, to hurt myself. We discussed the idea that it was a constant battle between two sides of me, but that I always had the choice. That night, I decided to try again to stop hurting myself. However, because I still hadn't sorted out my emotions or my reasons for hurting myself, the need to be drawn to self-destruction was still there. I started thinking about my weight an unhealthy amount of time.

Since I was about fourteen I had been overweight thanks to a hormone deficiency. This had always made me feel a little self-conscious, and I had been on many diets to try to lose some weight. But now, suddenly the idea of losing weight in a consciously unhealthy way appealed to me. I started taking laxatives every day. I'd have to go to different shops to buy them, so that people wouldn't recognize me and refuse to sell them to me. The desire to make myself thin (and subconsciously the desire to hurt myself) was stronger than the desire to be healthy. I tried not to think about what I was doing. By sixth form I started skipping breakfast, then lunch too. My friends all noticed, but because my parents saw me eating dinner they were actually encouraging me to lose more weight. My friends used to try to get me to eat: some would bring extra food in from home just for me. Others would just say quite forcefully, 'Sophie, go to the canteen and buy some food.' But I'd go and buy some lettuce and cucumber. I think a part of me liked the attention I got from my friends. I wanted people to know that something wasn't right. I didn't know *what* wasn't right – but I knew something wasn't. I lost a lot of weight quickly.

This continued for about a year, until one day a friend dragged me to the canteen to get some food. I looked at all the chips and burgers and they scared me. The thought of eating them, even touching them, sent shivers up my spine. But that fear, the fear of food, worried me even more. I was terrified about what road I was starting to go down, so I asked my two closest friends to help me to start eating and admitted to Bev that I was taking laxatives. Both Laura and Bev helped me to admit that I was trying to replace self-harm with a form of bulimia. When I started to eat healthily again and tried reducing my laxative abuse, the cutting and injuring came back.

5.

WHAT IS SELF-HARM?

Author's warning: The following chapter describes various self-harm acts and is very graphic. Please do not read it if you are squeamish or if you are a self-harmer.

It seemed that when I ceased one method of hurting myself, another would eagerly jump into its place. The self-harm spiral hadn't stopped; it had just taken on a different form. This pattern seems to happen to many self-harmers. If the underlying causes haven't been dealt with, it is very difficult to stop a destructive pattern once it has started.

The following is a list of methods of self-harm/destruction that have been used either by me personally or by fellow self-harmers who have been gracious enough to share their experiences with me. This does not cover all types of self-harm, and the real-life experiences that are shared are not necessarily the same for everyone. They are included in order to aid understanding. However, some of these are extreme examples and this list should not be used to dissuade anyone from admitting they are a self-harmer.

Cutting

This is widely acknowledged to be the most common form of self-harm. It can vary between scratching yourself with your fingernails to cutting deeply into your arm with a razor blade or knife, resulting in huge blood loss. This was the main form of harm I used throughout my years of hurting myself.

I have only a few scars on my body from cutting, because I was very vain and was conscious, even while I was in the act of cutting myself, that I did not want to have to wear long sleeves for the rest of my life. This meant that I rarely cut widely or deeply, but instead I would cut a lot. I would cut and cut and cut very quickly all over, so a typical 'session' could result in hundreds of cuts over my arms, legs and stomach.

Biting

Biting is rarely acknowledged as a form of self-harm, but many admit to doing it if there are no sharp implements available. I sometimes used to find myself biting my hand very hard when I was nervous or upset in public. It is something that was easy to do in communal settings because no one would notice or think it was strange. I would never break the skin, although some people bite down so hard they can take out an entire section of flesh.

Bruising/Bone-breaking

The line between what is self-harm and what isn't is not always clear-cut. It is seen as socially acceptable for a man, when stressed or upset, to punch a wall, even though that may lead to broken knuckles or even a shattered wrist. Many self-harmers will also punch walls, punch themselves, kick walls or use heavy objects such as sledgehammers, rolling pins or even Bibles to bruise themselves or break their bones. Some people may even throw themselves down the stairs or jump from heights to cause themselves damage.

Eating Disorders

Eating disorders and self-harm seem to have a hand-in-hand relationship. Many people who suffer from an eating disorder will also begin self-harming, and vice-versa. As I have already explained, I would regularly switch between self-harming and bulimia.

It seems to me that one of the reasons why these disorders are related is that they are both self-destructive coping mechanisms. They are also both things that someone can do to themselves without consciously hurting anyone else, or even needing anyone else to be aware of it. The development of other addictions such as alcoholism or even smoking can also be a form of self-harm. I started smoking when I was sixteen. None of my friends smoked, so it wasn't peer pressure, but I saw it as a way of hurting myself that no one would interpret as self-destruction.

Trichotillomania

Trichotillomania is the technical name for hair-pulling. Some psychologists argue that trichotillomania is not so much a form of self-harm as an obsessive-compulsive disorder. However, it is noted that many self-harmers also pull their hair out. People who injure themselves in this way may pull out sections of head-hair, eyebrows, eyelashes, pubic hair or any other hair on the body. Since many people pluck their eyebrows or wax their bikini lines, it must be made clear that people with trichotillomania are not plucking their hairs for aesthetic reasons but because it is an addiction.

Burning

Burning can involve putting out cigarettes on oneself, holding a naked flame against the skin, pouring hot water on one's skin or even sitting against a radiator with bare skin. I personally found burning a tempting prospect, and tried pouring hot wax on myself, but I didn't get the same comfort from it. Another form of burning which is quite rare but should be mentioned is freezing. I need to talk about this because it can be very dangerous.

When I was in my second year at university I found a wart on my thumb. I went to the pharmacist to see what was on offer to get rid of it before I tried the doctor, and found a product which was liquid nitrogen in a can. The purpose of it was to freeze the wart by applying a very small cotton bud covered in liquid nitrogen onto the wart for a few seconds. I bought the can, took it home and used it on my thumb. By this point at university I'd had some success in trying not to hurt myself. I hadn't done anything for ten months. However, I found this opportunity too hard to resist: it was something I'd never tried before and I was curious to see what would happen. So I froze a cotton bud and placed it on my skin. The bud gave me a very strange tingling sensation and also made a slight sizzling noise. It was not too bad, however, as when I lifted the cotton bud it had only left a pea-sized red mark on my arm.

The next day I awoke and saw that a little blister had replaced the red mark. It was mid-summer, and as it was no more than a small blister I reasoned I could explain it away. I went to my placement at a mental health centre, wearing a vest-top. When someone did ask me what I'd done, I said that I'd tried freezing my wart and a bit had dripped onto my arm. When I got home from work at lunchtime, the thought of freezing was still on my mind. I didn't want to blister myself or cause myself any permanent damage, for the same reason that I rarely cut myself deeply, so instead of using the liquid nitrogen I reached for a can of deodorant spray. I reasoned that it wasn't liquid nitrogen so it couldn't actually burn me, that it would just leave a red mark again.

I took the lid off and sprayed it onto my arm from a couple of millimetres away. I held it against my arm for minutes, just spraying and spraying until I'd used a whole large can of deodorant. I cannot remember what it felt like; I was busy admiring the patterns the spray was leaving on my skin when it solidified into a white powder before being washed away by the next wave of mist. When the can was empty I looked down at my arm and was shocked to see that my skin had turned solid. It looked and felt as though someone had placed a two-inch by five-inch piece of cold, white plastic on my arm. I panicked, because I had no idea how to treat it. I knew that if you burn yourself with something hot you need to run cold water on it for ten minutes, but I had never heard of someone burning themselves with something cold before. I held my other hand on my cast-skin for a few minutes to try to warm it up, until it felt more supple and soft, and then I timidly looked at it again. It no longer looked like plastic, but instead it now looked red-raw and was already blistering. I phoned the NHS Direct healthcare helpline to ask them what I should do. I told them I had frozen my arm accidentally with some liquid nitrogen in a chemistry lab. They told me to go to hospital immediately.

I determined I couldn't do that, because I was ashamed. But I knew I needed medical help, so I phoned my local doctors' surgery. I asked if I could see a nurse straight away, and after a bit of persuading they said I could. I texted a friend of mine called Bec and asked her offhandedly whether, 'as I was walking past her house to the surgery anyway', she could come with me. I didn't want her to know I was panicking and didn't mention in the text why I needed to go. Thankfully, she said OK, as she could do with a walk, and we set off.

As we were walking I told Bec that the liquid nitrogen can for warts was faulty and had leaked onto my arm. I lied to both her and the nurse, and said that the 'accident' had happened the night before, because this helped me to dissociate from the events. Projecting this lie into a previous day made it feel less real or prominent.

The burn was so bad that the nurse told me I should sue the company that made the liquid nitrogen. I had to visit the nurse every day for two months to get my bandages changed, because the blister on my arm was so big. After that I had to wear a scar-reduction dressing for another three months. It is still the biggest scar I have.

One of the hardest things about this incident was that the burn was so big and in such a prominent place on my forearm that everyone could see it. So everyone asked me what I'd done. I was so ashamed that I made up an elaborate lie that I told everyone, including my friends. I also made the lie slightly embarrassing – about warts – because I thought that if I did that, no one would question whether or not it was true. To this day, all my friends think that I hurt my arm with a faulty wart treatment.

'Night Walking'

This is the one method of self-harm over which I still feel shame. It is rarely talked about even within the self-harming community, and although many self-harmers think about it, few in reality, act on it. When I was in my first year at university, all the female students were warned by the police not to go to a certain area in the city late at night. There had been a number of incidents there involving a flasher in the previous months, and the area was also known for being a place where people had been raped.

Late one night I couldn't sleep and was feeling incredibly triggered, but I didn't feel like harming myself. It was an odd feeling that I hadn't experienced before, but although I wanted some form of damage to happen to me, I didn't want to be the person who did it. I decided to go for a walk around the area where we were told not to walk alone.

I wandered around, not actively looking for something bad to happen, but certainly not looking out for my safety either. It's hard to explain what was going on in my head at that time. I was thinking that it might be a good thing if I were attacked, that somehow it would be one 'big thing' that would erase an entire head of 'little things' that I had to deal with. I know that doesn't make sense, and that in fact if I had been attacked it would only have added to everything else that had happened to me, but that was how I was thinking at the time.

Thankfully nothing happened. When I reached a bridge that was the most dangerous spot, I saw a man standing alone, looking across the river. I froze for a second when I saw him. He looked up and started to walk swiftly towards me. I turned on my heel and sprinted home, cursing myself all the way for being such a stupid girl.

This type of self-harm isn't discussed, so it is hard to tell how often it happens or in what forms it can manifest. However, some people will go into town alone to pick a fight in order to get beaten, while others will enter into a violent relationship to be treated badly. Others, like me, will walk around dangerous areas waiting to be attacked.

Swallowing Dangerous Things and Overdoses

These are very important forms of self-harm which I feel I need to cover, as they can be extremely dangerous. Some self-harmers swallow things in order either to make themselves sick or to damage themselves internally. This can range from tissues to razor blades, to overdosing on drugs. Not all people who take intentional overdoses are trying to kill themselves. Although it might not be a suicide attempt, a self-harmer could still accidentally kill themselves if they adopt this practice. I used to take overdoses, mainly of paracetamol.

One evening, while I was in my first year at university, I was at the home of my college chaplain, John, babysitting his daughter Chloe. For the previous few days I'd been taking about ten paracetamol tablets each night. However, this evening I knew something worse was going to happen. It's strange, but I had a really good time babysitting Chloe. We played games and even went down to McDonald's to get ice cream. When John and his wife Megan came home, they gave me a box of chocolates as a thank-you for babysitting and we chatted for quite a while.

The sad thing is that at that point, chatting with John and Megan, I didn't want to go home. I was scared of going home, because of the feeling that I was going to do something worse than before. I didn't know what it was I was going to do, but I didn't trust myself. However, I was always too shy or embarrassed to tell people when I was feeling like this. Moreover, I was enjoying myself at John's house, and didn't want to change the mood by telling them I was worried what was going to happen when I got back to my room.

At about half past eleven I said goodbye to John and Megan and they closed their front door. When I was walking home I wanted to turn round and go back to John and Megan's, but I told myself I shouldn't keep them up when they wanted to go to bed, and I'd be fine anyway. So I kept walking.

When I got to my room, I closed the door and started to feel really fidgety. I couldn't sit still at all. I opened the box of chocolates and had a couple of caramels, then I tried playing solitaire on my computer before trying to read a book. I was still fidgety, so I decided it might be best if I went down to the college's common room to see who was around.

My college was fairly small, which was really nice because it meant that everyone knew everyone else. If there was anyone sitting in the common room, I'd know who they were and could hang out with them. But this time, when I got to the common room there was no one around. This was fairly unusual for my college, and because it was strange and my room-mate was away, a sudden feeling of loneliness filled me. I didn't know where anyone was because I'd been babysitting, and now I was all by myself. I was one of the helpers at the college shop, which meant I had shop keys. I let myself in and picked up two boxes of paracetamol, telling myself I could take a small overdose again. If I picked up two boxes I wouldn't have to go back again next time I wanted to take another small overdose.

I paid for the boxes and went back to my room. As quickly as possible I popped the pills out of their packets. There were twenty-two small white tablets on my bed sheets. As a result of various medical conditions, I've always had to take a handful of tablets every morning anyway, so I was used to taking a lot of pills without any problems.

I looked at them all. I picked them up, ran them through my fingers onto my pink skirt, then collected them again. There wasn't much going through my head except a negative voice daring me to take them. I felt myself encouraging myself just to swallow the whole lot. I picked up the stale glass of water I had by the side of my bed, clutched the pills in my right hand, put them all in my mouth, took a sip of water and swallowed.

As soon as I did, I thought, 'Oh my gosh, what have I done?' I knew it was too many. I'd read up on paracetamol and the side-effects of an overdose, and knew that although it wasn't enough to kill me it was definitely enough to cause some damage. I stood up and paced my bedroom, up and down, up and down. I wasn't sure what to do. I decided to text a friend of mine who lived on the floor below. I knew I had to go to hospital, but because I wasn't sure I wanted to, I texted, 'Hey Tom, how are you? If I had to go to casualty right now, would you come with me?' I honestly thought that that was a rather subtle question! After I'd texted it I continued pacing, wondering what I should do if he didn't get it soon or didn't text back. I sat on my bed and hugged my legs. I felt my heart miss a beat when I heard my phone beep and I got a text back from Tom. I picked it up and read: 'I'm just getting my coat.'

I panicked. Tom would come up to my room any second and take me to hospital. I would have to tell him what I'd done... I would have to tell the doctors what I'd done... What if they put me in a mental hospital? Could they lock me up? Were they going to pump my stomach? My mind was racing as I rushed to put on some make-up and get my coat. I thought I would need to look presentable and less crazy and disturbed if I was going to have to tell people I'd taken an OD. I'd just finished brushing my hair when I heard a knock at the door.

I didn't want to open the door. I was scared of the look I'd see on Tom's face. I didn't want to see him looking worried, because as far as I was concerned I didn't deserve concern: I'd done this to myself. My mind was still racing and I was still panicking, because when I did open the door to see Tom standing there I blurted out:

'I didn't say I had to go!'

Tom just walked in and gave me a hug.

'Right, so let's go get a taxi,' he said, sounding as though he was talking about grabbing something to eat.

'OK,' I agreed.

As we were walking down the road to the taxi rank, Tom asked me what I was dreading.

'Sophs, in case you suddenly drop down dead, or go unconscious or something right now, why are we going to casualty?' I knew that he needed to know, and would find out at casualty anyway.

'I've, er, taken an overdose,' I stammered.

'Right, OK: of what?' Tom covered his surprise fairly well.

'Paracetamol.'

'Ouch!' Tom continued walking. 'That's a nasty one.'

'Yeah, I know...' I was angry with myself. 'I'm an idiot.'

'Well, it's not the smartest thing to do,' he agreed.

When we got to hospital I went to the desk in casualty and the receptionist asked why I was there.

'I've er, overdosed,' I whispered. I cannot describe the look of disdain the lady gave me, except to say that it made me feel two inches tall. I received the same look from the triage nurse who saw me next. She took me to a cubicle immediately, which made me feel really guilty that I didn't have to join other people in the four-hour waiting time. Then another nurse came in with a friendly smile and gave me a plastic cup full of shiny black gloop.

'This is liquid charcoal,' she said apologetically. 'You're going to have to drink the whole thing.'

'What does it do?' I asked.

'Two things: it makes you throw up, and it coats your stomach so you can't absorb any more of the paracetamol. It doesn't just coat your stomach, though, but everything it touches. So I'd cover your clothes – make sure you don't spill it, OK?'

It was relieving to be cared for by this nurse. She even jokily warned me:

'It doesn't just coat things on the way in, by the way... For the next week or so *everything* will be black – just so you know, pet.'

The liquid charcoal didn't taste of much at all. It was the texture that was horrible. It felt like swallowing sand and slime mixed together, and the nurse was right about it covering everything. My teeth, tongue, gums, lips, everything it touched was black. I managed to swallow the whole thing in three large mouthfuls. The nurse said she was impressed that I'd managed it because most people started to throw up after one mouthful, although they'd still then have to swallow the rest too.

She left me and Tom alone in the cubicle. Tom asked me what I'd like to happen, and whether there was anything he could do. I said I'd like him to phone John, the chaplain, to let him know I was in hospital. He said:

'OK, but what do you want me to say?'

I thought for a moment and then replied, 'Let him know everything.' John was someone whom I considered to be a friend, and he was also my chaplain. I thought he would cope with the two o'clock in the morning phone call, and I really felt I needed someone older there with me who I knew cared about me. Tom walked out of the hospital to use his mobile.

I sat in the cubicle by myself and watched all the doctors and nurses walking past my door. After a short while, the triage nurse looked in on me as she walked past. I then heard a very loud conversation between her and another nurse I did not know.

'You know that girl who OD'd is in cubicle one?'

'The OD patient? Yeah, I know.'

'It's such a waste of our time having to look after stupid attention-seekers like her.'

'Yeah, but what ya gonna do?'

I sat there listening to them talk about me, knowing that they were speaking loudly on purpose so that everyone else in casualty would know what I'd done, to embarrass me. I felt completely humiliated and alone, but also extremely angry. I wondered how anyone who'd taken an overdose to try to kill themselves would have felt in the same situation as me and I was furious. I just couldn't believe that people in a caring profession like nursing could be so cold and malicious.

When Tom came back I told him what they had been doing. He said:

'Well I guess they're frustrated that they have to spend their time treating self-inflicted injuries when others come in with accidental problems. But if I hear them saying those things I'll have a particularly cross word.'

I asked Tom what had happened when he phoned John. He said John had told him he was getting up and dressed and would be there as soon as he could. I felt bad for waking John up, but I was really pleased he was coming.

When John arrived, Tom left us alone to talk. John came into my cubicle and sat himself down in the chair next to my bed and looked at me. He didn't say anything, he just sat.

'What is it?' I asked, not knowing what he was thinking.

'I've just left Megan at home really worried and concerned,' he said.

'I'm sorry.'

'No, I mean,' he tried again, 'I'm a chaplain for a college full of students; I've been in this position before. It's sad but true. But what really bothers both

Megan and me is that we didn't see this coming. I mean, we were with you this evening and you were smiling and joking as usual, and now... We just didn't see it.'

'No one ever does,' I said. 'I can't show people, I don't know how.' I tried to reassure him, but I knew that what I said was far from encouraging.

I had to stay in hospital for blood tests, so John took Tom home. It was just after they'd left that I started to throw up. Boy, did I throw up, every ten minutes for seven hours until eventually the doctors gave me a really painful injection in my backside to stop me gagging. For four days after drinking the charcoal I was so nauseous I couldn't eat anything.

6.

HOW TO HELP

'Self-harm' is the more common and preferred term for self-injury, although they are both commonly used. Self-harmers are often known by the abbreviated descriptions 'SI-ers' or 'harmers'. Self-mutilation is a term that has been rejected by most self-harmers, as mutilation is not the intention of the harm but can be the unfortunate side effect. Mutilation is also seen as a word that produces a sense of disdain which can make the already ashamed harmer feel even worse, whereas 'harm' seems a much gentler word.

Self-harm is used as a way of expressing deep anguish that the harmer may not feel can be articulated in words or sometimes even thoughts. As the information booklet *Understanding self-harm* published by mental health charity Mind (see Appendix for details) puts it, the self-harm can help the harmer to 'cope with feelings that threaten to overwhelm you; painful emotions, such as rage, sadness, emptiness, grief, self-hatred, fear, loneliness and guilt. These can be released through the body, where they can be seen and dealt with. Self-harm may serve a number of purposes at the same time. It may be a way of getting the pain out, of being distracted from it, of communicating feelings to somebody else, and of finding comfort. It can also be a means of self-punishment or an attempt to gain some control over life. Because they feel ashamed, afraid, or worried about other people's reactions, people who self-harm often conceal what they are doing rather than draw attention to it.'

The anguish is commonly caused by some form of trauma or painful experience that the harmer may not even know about. This is often something that happened to the harmer when they were a child or young adult. As Mind's booklet says, 'The experience might have involved physical violence, emotional abuse, or sexual abuse. They might have been neglected, separated from someone they loved, been bullied, harassed, assaulted, isolated, put under intolerable pressure, made homeless, sent into care, into hospital or to other institutions.' One result of traumatic experiences is low self-esteem and an absence of sensation: a numbness of emotions that protects the child from more pain but eventually causes them to feel very little.

One counsellor whom I saw explained to me that some people who have experienced trauma can convince themselves either that it didn't happen or that it wasn't a big deal. The result of this is that they start to find it very hard to see any occurrences as real or important. This gradually affects their self-esteem to the extent that subconsciously they can't see themselves as real any more, which is a scary place to be. The only way they can prove to themselves that they are real is through self-harm, either by feeling pain or by seeing blood. To quote Mind again, 'A badly traumatized person may end up feeling quite detached from their feelings and their body. Some may injure themselves to maintain that sense of being separate, and to convince themselves that they aren't vulnerable. Others may injure themselves in order to feel something and know that they are real and alive.'

It can be hard for self-harmers to explain how they are feeling when the desire to injure themselves is apparent, because they may be distant from the emotions. However, even if someone cannot feel emotions, it does not mean they are not there. The emotions still exist and need to be released somehow; this can be through harming. A common expression used by self-harmers when they want to hurt themselves is feeling 'triggered'. The only sensation I would feel tended to manifest itself physically rather than emotionally. The best way to describe it is as a tension that would build, high up in my chest. I could physically feel this tension, although I knew that it was an emotional pressure because I never thought there was anything physically wrong with my health. It was a horrible feeling that seemed to gradually build more and more, getting worse the longer I tried to ignore it, and the only way I knew how to rid myself of the heaviness was to 'cut it out' of myself.

It is usually hard to determine whether self-harm is occurring, as harmers normally hurt themselves in private and conceal or make excuses for any resulting marks. In the support group that I belong to on the internet, called busmail, there is an immense list of excuses that members can use if they are not yet ready to tell people why they have scars. These range from cat scratches to falling on barbed wire.

The pages that follow offer some things to remember when helping someone whom you know to be hurting themselves.

Christian Self-Harmers ARE Still Christians

For a long time, I thought I couldn't be a true Christian if I turned to my razor blades instead of to God for comfort. The reality is that self-harm is a sin just like every other one. It is wrong to do it, and it is important always to remember that God hates sin. But it is also imperative to remember that God loves, and through Jesus forgives, the sinner. I know God hated what I was doing to myself because it hurt him to see me hurting myself. He wanted me to cast my burdens onto him, and I know that he loved me too much to give up on me. Unless you have very strong doubts that the person engaging in self-harm acknowledges that self-harm is a sin, try not to question why they keep sinning, because this can increase their feeling of guilt and make them feel condemned.

However, do encourage them to pray and read their Bible when feeling triggered. This is so important. God can help a self-harmer not to hurt themselves, but often the harmer will not want to admit or recognize this fact.

I have asked many Christian self-harmers about their experiences with praying while feeling triggered. Here are some of their responses:

> 'On a few, very rare occasions, I have prayed when I felt triggered to self-harm. These occasions have been few and far between, however. Normally I will simply give in to the desire to self-harm and deal with the feelings later.'

> 'I will generally try to ignore the fact that God is with me during the entire act of self-harm.'

> 'I usually don't pray when I'm triggered because I'm just thinking about so many other things. The urge to SI is so intense that I usually block everything else out, including prayer. I do think about SI and God at times, but never when I'm triggered.'

> 'If there are times when I'm triggered and I really want to make an effort not to SI, I make myself pray, as this does help. If nothing else, it prevents me putting that gap between God and me. But

most of the time, SI is the only option I feel is going to make me feel better, so I don't honestly want to resist it, so I don't pray.

'When I do SI, I get God out of the equation as much as possible. I don't pray, I listen to anti-Christian music (e.g. Marilyn Manson) and if my mum's singing hymns I get out of earshot. I rarely think about him until well after I've hurt myself, perhaps the morning after. Then the guilt often kicks in, and I start thinking how I've failed yet again, how I'm a rubbish Christian, and how I'll never break free from this so I might as well stop trying now. Sometimes I apologize desperately to God, other times it distances me further from him as I don't want to face up to what I've done. I do believe SI is a sin, but that God wants to help us rather than being angry.'

For many self-harmers, part of the act of self-destruction is not to want help. The fact that wallowing in self-pity and melancholy can actually be enticing often means that many of us (whether or not we are self-harmers) can be drawn into the 'nobody loves me, everybody hates me' mentality and not want to be pulled out. For Christian harmers this often means they will try to ignore God or pretend that he doesn't exist while they are triggered. If you are with a harmer while they are feeling triggered, it can be really helpful to break the power of the melancholy by sensitively bringing God into the conversation. Asking the harmer if he or she would like you to pray for them is one effective way of encouraging them to recognize God's presence and power. Be aware, however, that this can cause some self-harmers to feel angry at you for breaking their self-destructive cycle.

Be There

I cannot stress enough how important others are when helping a self-harmer. Members of St Paul's and my friends at university have made my journey so much easier. Significant steps towards healing were made through them. They may not ever realize just how much help they've been to me.

If you are not a self-harmer but are concerned about a friend or member of your family who is, the most important thing that you can do is be there for them. Offer your time and a listening ear. Don't worry about whether or not you feel able to offer advice; it is far more important that you listen to them rather than talk to them.

My friend Carter, who has been such an amazing support for me over the years, said when discussing this:

'It is difficult for a non-self-harmer to understand the behaviour of a self-harming friend. I found it difficult to get my head around why someone would do something like that to themselves, how they would have started in the first place and why they can't simply quit. There was a strong temptation to bombard them with questions that just aren't helpful, as if it was poor old me that was upset and confused, needing the support from them.

'I still don't understand the mindset of a self-harmer completely, but in many ways that isn't important. I realized that the only things that mattered were that someone I cared about was in distress and that there was something I could do about it. I couldn't just make them stop; I couldn't make the hurt go away. But I could simply care for them, hold them close and accept them. If I could provide just a small island of calm in a sea of distress then that was something I would gladly do, whatever the cause of the distress.

'Sometimes I felt helpless, as if I should be able to do more to sort everything out, but there are no short cuts. All I could do was continue to love, support and pray for someone I cared about. As time went by, I gained a better understanding and got better at knowing how best to offer support.'

It is important that you understand how the self-harm makes someone feel. Do not feel the need to pretend that everything's OK if it's not. People have differing reactions to self-harm: some find it abhorrent, infuriating, alarming or confusing, and these are all understandable reactions. If you are finding it too hard to cope with, consider speaking to someone else for advice or support.

Keep Their Confidence

The shame and guilty feelings that can encompass a self-harmer can be huge, and so can cause the harmer to be very selective about who they tell their 'secret' to. This is something you need to respect as far as possible.

I write the following incident sensitively because it caused Andrew, Holly and me a lot of pain and discomfort in trying to sort it out, although I'm very glad to say that we have now succeeded. I decided to include this because I feel it is such an important issue when confidence is involved.

At university I would help to lead a youth group as part of my studies. One of the volunteers there was Andrew, with whom I got on very well. He'd accidentally found out about my self-harm one evening, but had become a great support to me from then on. When Andrew first discovered I was a self-harmer he found it hard to cope with. He'd never had anyone else confide in him about this type of issue before, and so felt overwhelmed. I didn't realize how badly he was taking my self-harm, and just how much of it he'd taken onto himself, otherwise I might have guessed what was going to happen. When Andrew started dating a girl called Holly I said that I'd love to meet her, so we decided to meet up one night. Holly was lovely, really friendly and chatty, and so as Andrew's friend I vetted and completely approved of his choice. As Andrew and I lived near each other, we walked home together. I started to tell him, tongue in cheek, about how I had decided to permit him to date Holly, when he suddenly looked at me seriously.

'Sophs, I was wondering if you'd mind if I told Holly about some of the reasons why you hurt yourself.'

'What?' I tried to process what this question meant.

'Well, I thought it could help Holly and me have a closer relationship if she knew how I was supporting you and why you hurt yourself.'

'What? She knows about... about...?' I couldn't say the words self-harm again.

'Well, she asked so I told her.'

'How did she ask?' I'd always been so careful about hiding cuts, and besides, I'd never even met Holly before.

'I don't know. She's fairly perceptive... I don't understand what the big deal is.'

'How many hints must you have given her for her to guess?' I couldn't believe that Andrew had done this. I'd trusted him and he didn't even understand that he'd betrayed my confidence in him. I never wanted to see him or Holly again.

So many thoughts ran through my head: Holly and I had spent the whole evening together and had got along really well; had she just been humouring me because she knew I cut myself? When we met I had no idea who she was, and vice versa, except that she already knew one of my deepest secrets. How dare she ask such a question about someone she didn't even know? Why did Andrew feel the need to tell her? Was I just a piece of gossip to him? I'd been smiley, happy and bubbly all evening, not knowing that he'd told her. Did I just look like a fool to them?

Andrew struggled with my self-harm and felt the need to talk to someone else about it for support and reassurance. Holly wanted to know what was happening in order to support her boyfriend. In fact there was nothing malicious about their intentions: they did care about me and I wasn't just some gossip to Andrew. But that is still how I felt at the time.

If a self-harmer has told you what they are doing to themselves, the number of people you tell should be kept to a minimum. Please note I am not saying that you should never tell anyone, but if you do feel the need to speak to someone else about the harmer you should always let him or her know first. I think if Andrew had asked, or even just told me he was going to tell Holly about my self-harm, I would have been nervous and unsure about it but I would have let him. It was the shock of him breaking my confidence in him behind my back that hurt the most – that and the idea that Holly knew this secret I kept, and yet I didn't know that she knew.

Look After Yourself

Caring for and being there for someone who hurts themselves can be both physically and emotionally draining. If you tried to be completely supportive to someone else all day, every day, you'd burn out and they wouldn't have any incentive to change. You have to find ways to be sure your needs are being met. Bev was a remarkable support for me over the years, and the way she managed to be there for me continuously was by not allowing herself to get caught up in my pain. This didn't mean she couldn't help me or that she couldn't empathize; in fact it meant she could help me more by staying grounded. She did this by setting rules as to when I could phone her and when I couldn't. I may have found this upsetting at first, but I got used to the rule and it helped us both.

Don't Blackmail the Harmer

Try not to make the harmer feel guilty. This may seem like an obvious 'don't', but it is far more common than people think. Simple phrases such as 'If you loved me you wouldn't do it,' 'It hurts me when you hurt yourself,' and 'Don't do it – for me?' are ones that every self-harmer hears often. So many times I tried to stop hurting myself for someone else, and every time I did that, I'd end up giving in eventually and cause myself even more damage than usual because of the guilt I felt for breaking my promise to that person. The only way a self-harmer can stop is for themselves and through God. It doesn't mean that they don't love you or care about you. It's an addiction that they struggle with and has nothing to do with their feelings for you.

Don't Take it Personally

The person you're concerned about is not self-harming to make you feel bad or guilty. Even if it feels like a manipulation, it probably isn't intended as one. People generally do not self-harm to be dramatic, to annoy others or to make a point. Try not to be offended or insulted if they do hurt themselves even when you've made every effort to help them not to.

If he knew I was triggered, my friend Andrew used to stay with me for hours into the early morning. His intention was essentially: 'Well, you can't do anything if I'm here, can you?'

And often it worked, because by the time he'd leave at around three in the morning, I'd be much calmer, and too tired, and would end up going straight to bed. However, sometimes even that wouldn't work and I'd just play along with him for those hours, pretending to be feeling better until he'd gone, and would then hurt myself. Again, it wasn't because he had done anything wrong. It wasn't because I didn't appreciate all his hard work for me and his care for me. It was because I was addicted to self-harm.

Don't Pretend It's Not There

It may be right to pretend you didn't see someone's scars if they are a stranger or an acquaintance, but if the harmer is someone who is close to you and you care about them, don't ignore their behaviour. If they admitted to you that they hurt themselves, try to see it as an honour that they felt able to tell you in the first place. If you happened to find out by accident, try to bring the subject up sensitively with them; let them know that you've noticed and you're willing to talk, and then follow their lead. If the reply is that they'd rather not talk about it, acknowledge this gracefully and drop the subject, possibly repeating that you're prepared to listen if they ever do want to talk about it.

Don't Be Afraid to Suggest Professional Support

The likelihood is that your friend or relative has already considered the idea of either speaking to their doctor or school nurse or going to see a counsellor, but may be too frightened. If you feel it could help, don't be afraid to bring up the idea of them seeing a professional, and offer to go with them. This could help the harmer to feel that their thoughts have been verified and give them more confidence to go.

I realize that some people may have read this chapter hoping for a simple, straightforward solution to helping a loved one stop hurting themselves. However, unfortunately the reality is that there is no single solution to 'save' a self-harmer, and it is important to remember that it isn't your job to save them. The pathway to stopping self-harming is normally long and difficult. Again, the most important thing I can stress to anyone who is concerned about a friend or family member who is hurting themselves is simply to be there for them. You will probably make mistakes in trying to care for them, but they will know that you are trying, and that's what they want. Do not be too afraid of upsetting them to try to care for them.

PAST REVELATIONS

As we saw in Chapter 6, it is assumed in most if not all self-harm situations that there is a traumatic event that caused it. However, the self-harmer does not necessarily know what this is and may not ever realize.

When I first started hurting myself I did not know why I felt compelled to do these things. I used to pray that God would show me why I felt I needed to hurt myself, because I honestly did not have a clue as to what triggered it. It wasn't until two years after I first began, when I was seventeen, that God revealed the trauma to me. The process of understanding the reasoning behind an action or a coping mechanism can take a long time, and this can be frustrating for the person involved as well as for the loved ones caught up in it. But patience is the best way to deal with it. God will reveal things to people in the best time and when, as well as if, he thinks they need to know.

It was a late Saturday morning and I had just woken up after having a typical teenage lie-in. I had recently left my Saturday drama school and was relishing the bliss of my first lie-in for years. I eventually got out of bed and went to have a shower. While I was in the shower I was daydreaming and thinking about past memories through my childhood. The revelation hit me like a ton of bricks:

I had been sexually abused by a female member of my family called Lucy.

I couldn't breathe. I fell down in the bath, threw up and then just sat under the shower head with the water trickling down me, hugging my legs, rocking. I wasn't crying, I was frozen, and I just sat there with wide eyes, trying to make sense of it all. I couldn't believe it. I didn't want to believe it. I felt really numb and flat. I think I must have sat there, curled up in the shower, for about an hour.

The strange thing is that the memories had always been there. They were not hidden; I had thought about them before. It was just that I had never allowed myself to see them for what they really were. I had somehow managed to block the effect of those memories without blocking the memories.

From the age of two until I was about twelve, this relative of mine had been abusing me. When I was two-and-a-half I was a very chatty, quite cheeky little girl. I'd talk to everyone and quite often say inappropriate things at the wrong time. When I came out of nappies, I was so proud of myself that I was telling everyone. When Lucy came to stay I told her I was wearing 'big girl pants', expecting to hear the usual 'Oh, well done!' that I'd heard from everyone else that day. Instead, she told me that she didn't believe me. I didn't understand why she said she doubted me, so I argued that I really was. She told me that she'd have to see for herself and put her hand up my skirt. She did not go inside my knickers, but she did touch me. I remember thinking that that was odd, but I think that at the time I was more confused about why she wouldn't just take my word for it than why she was doing what she was doing. That is my first ever memory. Unfortunately, many youth workers use within their youth groups a game which involves everyone saying their name and what their first memory is as a way of getting to know each other. Even before I had this revelation, I used to lie because I'd feel ashamed. I would tell everyone my second memory instead, saying it was my first.

Because she was female and a relative, my parents trusted Lucy to bathe me and get me ready for bed without their supervision until I was eight years old. It would mainly be in those times that she'd touch me. I never wanted her to give me baths, but because she was an adult and it was rude to say no to adults I never complained. Nothing would happen during the bath time; it was afterwards that was the problem. I'd stand up in the bath and, just like my parents did, she'd wrap me in a big towel, lift me out of the bath and carry me into my bedroom. It was then that I'd start to feel nervous, and so because I didn't like what was going to happen next, I would ask her if she'd let me dry myself,

because 'I'm a big girl now, I can do it all by myself.'
To which she'd always reply:

'No, you won't do it properly. I need to do it.'
When she said this, I would pull away.

Looking back on it now, I think that that was the
worst part. When I pulled away she'd let me. I would
end up standing in the corner of my bedroom, naked,
dripping wet and shivering cold, while she'd sit on my
bed and just... wait. Very occasionally, she'd pull me
back, give me a smack and tell me to stop being
naughty, and one time she threw the towel at me,
called me a stupid girl and stormed out. But almost
always she'd just wait.

I would stand there, adamant that I was not going to
go back to her, when from downstairs I'd hear my
parents and brother laughing at something on the TV or
just chatting together, and I'd think to myself, 'The
sooner I get this over and done with, the sooner I can be
warm in my nightie and downstairs with them.' I also
thought that I was being naughty for not doing as she
said and for arguing with her, and I would worry that
she'd tell my parents. So I'd give in and go back to her.

While drying me, Lucy would go between my legs
and touch me, usually with the towel only covering part
of her hand. She would also 'dry' inside me and put
talcum powder on her fingers and rub it everywhere on
my body.

I remember this happening many times. The reason
I never told anyone about what was going on was
because I thought it was normal and that I was being

bad when I argued or struggled. I reasoned that she was just drying me, and that if I didn't let her and if she or I told my parents they'd be cross with me. I remember clearly one night when I was six. I had pulled away from her and was standing in the corner of my room when I thought to myself, 'Pulling away makes things worse. Being frightened or angry isn't helping, so I'll stop feeling those things.' I couldn't control what was going on, but I could control how I managed the resulting emotions. From then on I never pulled away or felt any emotions during those sessions. It felt as though I had a switch to my feelings that I could flick on or off any time I needed to. It was a preservation mechanism that this small six-year-old child developed to look after herself during those times.

All this had an effect. When I was fourteen I used to help my ballet teacher teach her youngest class. The class contained around fifteen three-year-olds. I loved teaching them. I remember all of us sitting in a circle with our feet in the middle, saying 'Good feet' when we pointed our toes and 'Bad feet' when we pulled them up again. My favourite part of the lesson was when we told the children they could go and get changed back into their normal clothes. They would run over to the chairs where their bags were and routinely strip off their leotards and proceed to run around the room completely naked. At first my teacher and I would try to stop them doing this, but we decided it was a losing battle and eventually just let them. As their parents started coming in to collect them, the children would all scream and say, 'Oh no, we've got no clothes on!' and run back to the chairs – and the first item of clothing they'd put on would be their socks! Not their knickers, not their vests, but their socks. The parents would laugh and everyone thought it was very cute.

I used to love seeing their innocence. I reasoned that the parents had at some point probably told them that it isn't a good thing not to wear clothes in public, and their children had taken that on board, but did not understand what it really meant. The fact that these children were so uncorrupted by the world was something that I looked forward to seeing every week. Yet something about that whole situation also used to sadden me a bit. I had started ballet when I was two years old, but I could not remember sharing that innocence. I always knew what bits little girls need to cover up, and I felt that I knew it too well. At fourteen, I was hurt for the little girl inside me who'd had that innocence taken away from her.

When my family went to stay with Lucy, I'd have to stay in her room and she would often undress in front of me and expect me to undress in front of her too. I always tried to hide and turn away when she did this, but I never complained. When I was nine, on Christmas Eve in the morning I woke up at about seven o'clock and asked her if I could go downstairs and watch cartoons. Lucy told me that I should stay upstairs because she didn't want me to wake my parents. I told her that they were deep sleepers and never minded when I went downstairs to watch TV at home.

'Just stay up here with me for a while. You can go downstairs in a bit,' she encouraged, then proceeded to tickle me and hug me. She told me to get into bed with her for a cuddle and switched off her bedside clock, saying that it was too bright. While lying in bed, I would ask her when I could go downstairs.

'Soon,' she'd reply.

We lay in bed, with her alternating between stroking me and sleeping, until I heard some noise outside my bedroom. Seeing it as a great excuse to get out of the bed, I jumped up and ran to the door to open it. It was my uncle.

'Morning! I thought you would be downstairs with your brother watching cartoons. I was just coming to join you,' he said. I loved my uncle: he was so much fun and very funny.

'Morning, what time is it?' I asked

'It's just past eleven o'clock,' he replied.

I just looked at Lucy, who was by now sitting up in bed, and walked out.

As I got older, the bathing stopped. I assume this was because it would have looked suspicious or because I was getting old enough to question it. However, whenever Lucy visited or we visited her, she would insist that if I was having a shower or bath I did not lock the door in case I 'slipped over and broke my neck'. This would mean that most times I showered or bathed she'd 'forget' that I was in there and walk in. She wouldn't do anything to me: she'd just stand and look.

She would also grope me while she was giving me a hug and touch my bottom whenever she was walking behind me.

One time when I was thirteen, Lucy came to visit us and I had to share a room with her. While I was asleep, I awoke to find her standing over me, holding my nose and covering my mouth – preventing me from breathing. I started to panic and struggle, but as soon as she saw that I'd woken up she stopped what she was doing and casually walked back to her bed. I asked her why she'd done it and she replied that she was worried that I'd stopped breathing in my sleep and was just checking that I still was. The next night while I was asleep she slapped me around my head, and when it woke me she said that I had hair in my face and she was trying to get it away. The night after that, again, she slapped me hard around my head when I was sleeping at four in the morning. This time she simply asked me if I had any paracetamol, because she had a headache. I said I'd go and get her some. I was tired because each night, once she'd woken me, I was too scared to get to sleep again. I brought her up some paracetamol and a glass of water, then lied: I told her I'd forgotten my own glass of water, so went back downstairs, curled up on the sofa and cried myself to sleep.

For the rest of the week that Lucy was staying I faked a cough which I told everyone was worse at night. So 'because I didn't want to wake Lucy up with my coughing', I excused myself from my bedroom and slept on the sofa instead.

Since I had grown up with this treatment, it didn't seem unusual to me. This was one of the reasons why I'd never thought about what had happened. I also didn't want to admit what had happened. For years after the moment of revelation I would seesaw between believing that Lucy had abused me and believing that she couldn't have abused me, and that it must have been me who was sick and perverted for ever thinking that she could do such things. I didn't want to believe it was true because it was too painful, and it was also less common because she was female.

After the revelation I got out of the shower, put on my dressing gown and went back to my bedroom. Still feeling dissociated, I took some of the cuddly toys I'd had when I was a child from the top shelf of my bookcase and put them on my bed. I then got into bed and wrapped the duvet round me, surrounded myself with the toys and curled up into a ball. I lay there staring into space for a long time until I fell asleep.

When I woke nearly two hours later, I felt a little more like myself again. I was still feeling extremely fragile, but I felt able to function. I got dressed and had some lunch, then went back up to my room and thought about what had happened that morning. I knew that I couldn't dismiss what had just taken place, even though I was very tempted to. I decided that I needed to tell Bev, because I knew that I would ignore the incident if I didn't. The only problem was I didn't know how to. I gave her a call and asked if I could go round to her house for a chat. I think Bev could tell there was something important I needed to tell her through the sound of my voice, because when I went round, instead of just chatting as I helped her make tea for her kids, she gave her children games to play upstairs and we sat in her living room. She asked me what was wrong, but I had no idea how to tell her about Lucy. I was worried that she wouldn't believe me. Bev was really good and listened to me waffling on about school and making jokes for about an hour because I couldn't bring myself to start the process of telling her, until eventually she asked me:

'So, Sophie, what did you really want to talk to me about?'

I could feel my heart starting to pound through my chest and my breathing got shallower, but I tried to stay calm and reminded myself that Bev loved me and wanted to help.

'You know we've talked about trying to work out what triggered me to start all this in the first place?' I said.

'Yes.'

'Well, I think I might know what it is.'

'What is it?'

'Well...' I couldn't bring myself to say the two words 'sexual abuse'. It's odd, but even to this day I find those two words really difficult to say.

'You know in the past I've mentioned what seems to be the most common trigger for self-harm?'

'Yes.' I think Bev realized I was struggling and so wanted to be as gentle as possible.

'I know it sounds strange me telling you now, but I think... I'm not sure, but I think it could be that.'

'Someone sexually abused you?'

'Possibly.' I still didn't want to admit it.

'Is it still happening now?'

'No.'

'Who was it?'

'Er...' I didn't want to say. I didn't think she'd believe me: who would? Lucy was a sweet lady whom everyone loved. The only bad thing that people saw in her was that she was too caring; overly fussing around people. I found it hard to believe me, so how could anyone else?

'I'm worried you won't believe me.' I started crying. This was harder than I'd thought it would be.

'Why would I think you were lying about something like this?' Bev asked.

'I don't know.'

'So try me.'

I told Bev who it was I thought had hurt me as a child and she listened. I think she was shocked, but she hid it well because she didn't really react. Bev told me I was very brave for telling her and she gently told me that because of her responsibilities as a youth worker she needed to tell her leader at St Paul's, Ruth. I said that she could but that I'd want to know as soon as she did, and what was said and how Ruth reacted. I wanted to know every bit of information about the meeting because it somehow made me feel safer.

111

Bev then asked if we could pray, and through my tears I said that would be good. She started praying, thanking God that he was with us right there and then, supporting both of us and comforting me. She thanked God that he'd given me the strength to tell her and prayed that he'd give her the wisdom to know what to do with the information. She then asked me if I wanted to say anything. We sat in silence for a long time because I didn't know what to say to God. All of this was so new to me and I was finding it difficult. Eventually I decided to talk in tongues because then at least I knew that I was praying what needed to be prayed; even if I didn't know what it really meant.

After I'd had my moment of revelation I felt very fragile and vulnerable. I was quieter at school and with my friends. I had recently become very good friends with a girl called Laura, and she was fast becoming my best friend. We went on Christian camps together and would pray together. She was the first person who noticed I wasn't eating and whom I told that I was taking laxatives. Laura noticed that I was more withdrawn, and asked me what was wrong and whether I wanted to chat. I had been dismissing her questions for a while, but finally realized that she really did care about me and wanted to help. For a few days I tried to figure out whether or not to tell her about my childhood, and even when I'd decided to tell her, I didn't know how to.

Finally I determined to write Laura a letter. I just wrote that I really appreciated the fact that she cared for me and that I wanted to let her know because I trusted her. I still found it hard to write 'sexual abuse' or any similar words, so I simply wrote that Lucy had 'done things to me that she shouldn't have' and left it at that. When I saw Laura at school during a free period, I told her I'd like to take up her offer of a chat. We found an empty classroom and grabbed a couple of seats at the back. As quickly as possible, so I wouldn't have to think about it, I took the letter out of my bag and handed it to her. She took it from me, slightly confused, and started to read it. I sat there, biting my nails and watching her face, trying to read any change in expression. Halfway through her reading I started panicking and wanted to snatch the letter from her, rip it into hundreds of pieces and burn them. I actually had to sit on my hands to prevent myself from stopping Laura reading. After what felt like a lifetime, she finished. Without a word, she folded up the letter, looked at me, stood up and gave me a hug.

I asked her what she thought.

'I really don't know what to say.'

'What on earth do you think of me?' I asked her.

'Nothing's changed. You're the same Sophie in my eyes as you were before I read the letter.'

I felt so thankful that Laura wasn't disgusted with me: that was the biggest fear I'd had when telling her. It was really hard for me to believe that anyone could not see me as dirty and foul. She helped me feel more confident about speaking out about what had happened.

Both Bev and Laura suggested I see a counsellor, because neither of them felt qualified to give me advice about dealing with sexual abuse. Although I was really nervous about it, I decided that this sounded like a good idea. I found a Christian counsellor called Amy through St Paul's and I started seeing her. I was really nervous talking to my counsellor, and to be honest she was not competent in handling my problem. I have seen another counsellor since then and he was really good, so I truly don't want to put anyone off seeking counselling – if you're self-harming it can be a helpful thing to do. I would never try to dissuade anyone from seeking professional help, but for me I found it obstructive at that point.

When I was taking laxatives, I decided to try to tell her, and her reaction was:

'Well, ten laxatives a day isn't that bad; one of the clients I used to see took sixty a day!'

This did not help me at all. It made me feel as though I needed to take more laxatives and damage myself more to prove that I had a reason to feel bad, which was not a good thing to think. It felt as though Amy was either trying to get me to compete in severity with her other clients or was belittling what I was going through. I found myself becoming very self-defensive when I was with her and not wanting to talk to her at all.

One evening, about two months into seeing Amy, I was chatting with Bev and she asked me if I had told her about the abuse. I said I hadn't yet, so Bev asked me if I'd like her to come with me to encourage me. I told her that I'd try in the next session by myself first, and if I still couldn't I'd ask her to come with me after that.

At the next session I decided to tell Amy about what used to happen to me when Lucy gave me a bath. Because I was still trying to deny the reality of the incidents, I told her that although I knew what occurred really did happen, I was worried that maybe it was all completely innocent and that I'd put some twisted, tainted view onto it that wasn't really valid.

Amy told me that I'd obviously misinterpreted the situation. She said:

'Standards of hygiene are not the same today as they were when she was young, so maybe she just thought she needed to dry you that way. Women very rarely abuse children like that; it must have been a misunderstanding. I mean, she didn't physically hurt you, did she?'

I was completely taken aback by what Amy said. I didn't want to say any more. So I simply said:

'Yes, you're right. I must've just misinterpreted it.'

We spent the rest of the session looking at why I might have misread what had happened. I remember thinking to myself, 'You're a professional counsellor; you're supposed at least to pretend you believe me if I say something like this. If you can't believe me, how on earth could anyone else?' It made me feel humiliated and depraved. I agreed with everything she said and walked home feeling completely numb, lost and confused. Amy and I had arranged to meet for another session the same time the following week, but I didn't show up. I lied to Bev and Laura and said that Amy and I had finished our sessions. I never went back to see her again.

I didn't talk to anyone about Lucy for two years after that day.

BULLYING

When I left school I tried to reduce the amount I was hurting myself, and I managed quite successfully. When I started my gap-year job as an assistant youth and children's worker, I decided I couldn't hurt myself while I was in this role. I reasoned that if one of the children or young people I worked with found out, it could really hurt them. I think it was this determination to be professional, and just being able to see it as a non-option, that meant I kept to my decision and didn't hurt myself.

However, although I was working for a church, it was very difficult for me to do the job because I was bullied by the children's worker, Robert. Later I heard theories from his friends that he'd been in love with me but had treated me badly to try to negate his feelings because I was eighteen and he was thirty and married. Rob would be very rude to me, sabotage my work, blame me in front of everyone for minor errors in my written work, make me work longer hours than the other two assistants and then reward them for working hard by taking them on holiday, leaving me behind to keep working. He just generally made my life as hard as possible. I didn't want to leave, because I loved working with youth and children, but I couldn't cope with the way he treated me. I prayed to God, asking him whether or not I should quit my job. Every time I prayed this prayer, I felt God giving me the same response: that I should stay where I was, because he was bigger than all of this, and he was going to bring glory out of it.

So I stayed. Things continued to get worse at the church, St Joseph's, but whenever friends or family asked me how things were going I told them how brilliant it was. I was ashamed of being bullied, but also I really did like the parts of my job that didn't involve contact with Rob. But then one day, as I was using one of the church's computers to email my best friend Laura, I cracked and told her I thought Rob was 'scum'. I said that he'd ignore me for days at a time, 'which I wouldn't mind except I need to work with him', and that he'd insult me as a 'joke' or even physically threaten me. I felt better telling Laura about what was going on. It was good to know that someone else knew how I was feeling. But what I didn't know was that Rob had been hacking into my emails and reading them. He printed out my message to Laura and gave it to the vicar, Neil, who then fired me.

Neil invited me and a gracious lady, Julie, who'd recently been assigned to me as my mentor, to his house, where the children's worker was already waiting. Neil explained that Rob had 'accidentally' found the email I'd sent to Laura and that obviously things weren't working out, so it might be best if I left. He then gave the floor to Rob, who said:

'We've been concerned about the tension in the office for quite a while, and I think this will be the best solution all round. You haven't always worked to your highest performance, and that's to the detriment of the work of St Joseph's. I have also had a few complaints about your behaviour with some of the younger children being inappropriate.'

I was so upset that I asked if Julie and I could step outside for a minute, which we did. When we closed the door behind us I was ready to collapse. However, Julie wouldn't let me. She said:

'No, you can do that when we get you home. We're going to go back in there and ask questions.' So we sat down in the kitchen and she drew up a list of things that she would ask if I felt I wasn't able to. I had a glass of water, Julie made me take a few deep breaths, and then we went back into the living room and sat down.

'Sophie has some questions about some of the things that Rob said,' Julie told Neil and Rob, and gave me a nudge in my side.

Then I stood up for myself. I brought up all the things that Rob had been doing to me and described how he was degrading me and treating me really badly. Julie and I also showed that Rob's accusation of complaints against my treatment of young children was completely made up, and that the reality was that there were allegations about him having inappropriate relationships with teenage girls.

But even though all this had happened, I had already been asked to leave. Neil could not go back on that decision, and I would not have wanted to go back to work there. Julie took me home, and I went to bed and cried all night. Neil phoned me the next day and invited himself round to my house, where he apologized to me for everything that had happened. He told me he wished I'd told him these things before it had gone so far.

As soon as I had left St Joseph's and moved back into my parents' house I started hurting myself again. Because of what had happened with Rob I stopped calling myself a Christian. I blamed God for what had happened, because it hurt and because I'd been praying about leaving. I'd kept asking God whether I should leave but it had seemed he was telling me to stay, and then I'd ended up being fired in a horrible and humiliating way. I told everyone that I no longer believed in God. Because of this, I no longer cared that I was hurting myself. I was angry: angry with God and Rob and Neil, and with myself for being bullied. I needed to take out my anger on someone, and the easiest and closest person was myself.

Neil phoned the vicar at St Paul's to let him know what had happened. He told him that he felt 'like a shepherd who's lost a sheep'. He was worried that I was going to stop going to church, and he was right. I didn't want to go to church: as far as I was concerned I didn't care about God any more because he didn't care about me. As I wasn't that close to the vicar of St Paul's, he contacted the new curate, Nat, and his wife Helen, with whom I was very good friends, to let them know. Nat emailed me and asked me why I'd stopped going to church.

I told him that I didn't believe in God any more. Nat pursued this and asked, 'Is there a specific reason for you no longer believing, or is it just a general feeling?'

I replied, 'It's a general feeling. And even if I do believe in God, I don't care any more.' I knew, deep down, that I still believed. I couldn't lie about that. I just didn't want to believe any more.

Nat spoke to the leaders of St Paul's and then invited me to go on a weekend away with the church for free. His actions made it clear that he wanted to help me. He emailed me three times even though I was planning to see him that evening, and as I was emailing him a reply message he tried phoning me, but when I got to the phone he'd hung up. So I then tried to call him back, but his phone was engaged because he was emailing me again! I wasn't sure if I wanted to go on the weekend away, but I felt amazingly cared for – there were people who were so determined to make sure I was OK. That evening I visited Nat and Helen. Helen asked me:

'You don't think we're trying to get rid of you this weekend, do you? I think Nat's been a bit over the top, and I was worried you might think it's because we don't want you around.'

Nat interrupted. 'It's not that, it's just I really think this weekend would be good for you.'

The weekend was about prayer and praise. Part of me felt quite strange to be going on it, especially as no one there knew that I'd given up on God. But I was still enjoying being with some of my friends. Before I went, Helen encouraged me to be open and willing to deal with the things that had happened at St Joseph's. I wasn't sure, but I thought I'd see if I could try. One thing happened which I definitely recognized even then as God's intervention. I had volunteered to help lead the worship for the weekend, but as I travelled down to the destination I completely lost my voice. My whisper was actually louder than when I tried to speak, and this lasted until the Monday morning, when suddenly my voice came back. God didn't want me to lead the worship when I wasn't planning on worshipping him. He also wanted me to start to deal with some of the issues I had with him, instead of being distracted by singing.

On the Saturday night, everyone was together singing praises to God, and I was sitting in the corner at the back, just watching. No one questioned why I wasn't involved with the singing, because I obviously had no voice. As I was sitting there I decided that maybe I should try to speak to God about not trusting him any more because of how I felt he had treated me at work. Eyes open, still watching everyone sing, and smiling just in case anyone turned round to see me, I started shouting at God in my mind and asking why he hadn't told me to leave my job.

'You could have saved me from all that, but oh no, you let me stay there, thinking that everything was going to get better because you're in control, and then I was fired. I was stupid, yes. I didn't tell anyone about what was going on, but you told me to stay. I was thinking about leaving, I would have left, but instead I had my insides torn out and I was kicked out!'

I carried on praying, but God seemed so far away. I'd thought that maybe if I opened up to him, he would show me exactly why this had happened, and that I'd realize I was wrong for blaming him, I'd apologize and we'd 'make up'. But this didn't happen. I didn't feel any different, and God didn't answer. Tears started rolling down my face. I couldn't hide it. Heather, the children's worker at St Paul's, noticed me, came over and sat with me. She asked me what was wrong and I tried to explain, but because I could only whisper she couldn't hear me over the music. So we went back to my bedroom and I told her about everything that had happened at St Joseph's. Heather and I prayed together, although I still didn't feel that God was answering. She then asked me whether I'd like to meet up with her once a week for a chat. I said I thought that'd be a good thing.

Over the next few weeks Heather listened to me complaining about Rob and the way I was treated by St Joseph's and how bitter I was. When I was telling her one of my stories about how Rob had wronged me, eventually she said:

'Sophie, you've told me this before. If you feel you need to tell me again, then I'll listen again, but I already know it.'

I thought for a second, but still wanted to repeat the story. I was so bitter and angry; all I was thinking about was Rob's treatment. I couldn't stop thinking about it; I was dwelling on it all day, every day. I admitted this to Heather and she told me that for the following week she wanted me to write down every single thought I had about Rob on a small piece of paper, fold it up, store it in a bag and bring it back when I next saw her.

I tried this and wrote down every thought about Rob that I had. I even thought of a few more things about him to write down and show to Heather. I had started strangely enjoying dwelling on the negative things that had happened and I got quite excited about showing Heather all these things that Rob had done to me.

The next week I turned up at Heather's house and she had a fire burning in her living room. I guessed that this was to burn my scraps of paper. Heather told me that we were going to sit down by the fire, I was going to bring out my bag of paper, and one by one I was going to throw each piece, still folded up, into the fire. Each time I threw one in, Heather was going to read out a truth about me.

I took out my little plastic bag and looked at all the pieces of paper. I didn't like the idea of burning them, especially not being able to read them one last time before doing so. Heather and I sat looking at the fire for a long time, not saying a word. I alternated between looking at the fire and at my bag of paper. I wasn't thinking a lot; I was mainly just delaying having to burn these memories. Eventually I decided I needed to throw the first one in quickly, so I hurriedly picked out one slip and, without giving myself time to think about it, threw it into the flames.

'You are a child of God,' Heather said. I took a deep breath: it was really good to be reminded of that as I watched the memory burn away. I took another fragment and threw it into the heat.

'You are an heir to the kingdom of heaven.'

And another.

'You are fearfully and wonderfully made.'

The action became easier as each little white scrap of folded paper disappeared into the fire, until eventually the whole bag was empty. I didn't feel any different. As far I was concerned at that moment, nothing had changed. But when I was walking home from Heather's that evening I started to think about Rob again and suddenly stopped and thought, 'I can't think about that any more: I've burnt it.'

The thought surprised me, but I was so pleased. What had happened with Rob was unfair and painful and I didn't need to deny that, but I also didn't need to dwell on it any more. It's amazing how a small action like that changed how I felt about Rob. Over the next couple of weeks I talked with Heather about feeling that God had let me down, and I explained to her how I had prayed and asked for guidance and felt as though he had given me wrong advice. Nat had told me when I first saw him that in his opinion suffering happens for three different reasons – sin, Satan and stupidity – and that all three were at work in this case. I thought that was true: Rob's sin, Satan's temptation, and my naivety in not realizing Rob was in love with me and in thinking that keeping quiet about his treatment was the best idea. But what I still couldn't understand was why God had told me to stay.

Heather suggested that the allegations about Rob had needed to come out, and that while I was staying quiet that wouldn't have happened. St Joseph's had been suffering with secrets, mainly in the congregation, but this was a very big one within the staff team and God didn't like secrets. She also suggested that sometimes God needs us to learn that his way is always the best, even if it hurts. It made sense. I realized that God needed to use me to show what was happening with Rob. I offered all this up to God that evening and felt him with me again. I repented of not trusting him and of blaming him, and I felt completely forgiven and loved. God also showed me that during the weekend away, while I was feeling that he wasn't answering my prayers, he already had done, through Heather. Yet again I learnt that he was always there and had never given up on me, even when I had on him.

9.
CHANGE

During the summer of my gap year I went on a Christian camp in Somerset as a helper. The camp was run by Nat and was aimed at enabling young people from all walks of life to spend ten days away from home, play very silly, messy games and learn about God. As a helper, my job was to serve food, wash up, clean toilets and generally help out – and pay for the privilege. It was tremendous fun – I'd recommend it to anyone. All the helpers got a house to ourselves and we'd stay up really late, playing silly games and talking. It was there that I met Carter, a young maths teacher from York. Carter was also a helper at the camp, and we got on really well. It was unusual, especially as I had only just met him, but I felt I could trust Carter right from the start. As well as the joy of cleaning toilets, the helpers had some in-depth Bible studies together, which was amazing. The depth of knowledge that some of the 'helper leaders' had was awesome. One evening we were studying sex, and the fact that it was a truly wonderful gift from God, that two people who were married could share such a powerful bond with one another and be 'made one' in the process. Although I knew all this already, it really took me aback this time: it reminded me about Lucy and I couldn't get the thoughts out of my head.

All the helpers had to perform a sketch to everyone at the end of the camp, and we decided to perform 'Mop Right Now', a song that Carter, my friend from home, Hannah, and I had written. We were up until fairly late choreographing the dance that everyone had to learn. In the end Hannah said that she was going to go to bed. I was still feeling really vulnerable about what had been discussed in the earlier Bible study and was worried I would have bad dreams, so I wasn't ready to go to bed and told Hannah that I'd be up soon. Carter seemed to be able to tell that something was bothering me, which surprised me because no one else ever could. When Hannah went upstairs he asked me what was wrong.

'Oh, nothing,' I replied as casually as possible. I hadn't spoken to anyone about Lucy since the incident with my counsellor two years before.

'Well, is there anything I can do?' he asked.

'No, really,' I said.

'Are you sure?'

'Well, you could give me a hug,' I replied.

'Thought so.' He smiled, sat down next to me and gave me a hug. I felt so much safer with Carter just sitting next to me like that, but still not better. We sat together for a while in silence while I tried to distract myself from thoughts about Lucy. I'd read about how to stop flashbacks a while before, when a friend of mine had been suffering from them, so I tried those tactics. While still with Carter, I looked round the room and tried to count things that would add up to ten. This is not as easy as it sounds, and the idea is that it distracts you from other thoughts.

'Nine!' I said aloud, frustrated.

'What are you doing?' Carter inquired.

I explained that I was trying to distract myself by playing a game.

'From what?' he asked.

For some reason I wasn't as scared that he wouldn't believe me as I thought I would be. It also didn't worry me that I had only known him a week. I told him:

'A relative of mine called Lucy used to abuse me when I was little. I sometimes need to distract myself from thinking about it and getting flashbacks.' It came out so easily.

'OK,' he said. 'Tell me the game, then.'

He believed me, simply. He didn't try to get me to say anything I didn't want to. He didn't push me away and think I was a freak. He just stayed and supported me. We then spent a couple of hours looking round the room, counting things and making silly, not-at-all-funny jokes about how we could cheat and pretend there were more chairs or fewer chair legs in order to get up to ten. This carried on until eventually I felt OK and able to go to bed. Carter and I have remained really good friends since the camp and often travel to visit each other.

Carter helped me to realize that in fact it was more likely than not that people would believe me concerning what had happened with Lucy. However, this sometimes caused problems, because I didn't always believe myself.

The power of denial can be a very authoritative force, even when you know that something has happened. As I mentioned before, I always remembered what Lucy had done to me, which was never questioned in my mind. But I would often have doubts as to what her intention could have been. I didn't want to believe that what had happened to me was abuse. I often prayed that God would let me know, somehow, whether or not it was abuse, but never felt him answer. So I'd find myself telling Carter reasonably, calmly and honestly about things Lucy had done, and then suddenly flying off the handle and denying that Lucy had meant to do any of those things. I would repeat the words of my counsellor and say that I'd misinterpreted it all, and tell Carter that he shouldn't listen to me because I was 'obviously just some sick, twisted pervert'. I would start to panic and pace up and down in front of him, telling him to forget everything I'd said, justifying it:

'Lucy's a lovely person; everyone loves her, and she's wonderful. She couldn't do something like this. It's me. I'm scum. I'm horrible and fat and ugly and...'

The more worried I became about saying bad things about Lucy, the more insulting I would be about myself. This would carry on until Carter simply stopped me speaking. He didn't have anything to say, but he didn't need to. Just his presence helped more than words could anyway.

When my gap year ended I went to university to study to be a church youth worker. The self-harm was still a part of my life, but it had changed from a very regular occurrence to infrequent but more destructive incidences. The overdose, the burn on my arm and the risky walk at night all happened while I was at university. Most of my friends knew that self-harm was something I had done in the past, and I think that although we rarely spoke about it, those who knew this also realized that I sometimes still slipped back into the habit. One time a girlfriend of mine called Sarah was playing with my hair when she noticed some faded cut-marks on my arm. She poked them and asked:

'What are they?'

I knew there was no way I could pretend they were anything other than what they were, so I just said:

'Oh, I cut myself.'

'Sophs!' Sarah brushed my hair slightly harder and sounded a bit cross, but that was it. She didn't feel she needed to say any more, and in fact I was pleased at her reaction. It showed that she cared about me, because she didn't like the fact that I'd hurt myself, but she also didn't make it into a much bigger issue than it was.

After I had taken the overdose that left me in hospital, I invited myself to stay with Nat, the curate at St Paul's, and his wife Helen for a few days, to get away from university. I didn't tell them about the overdose when I asked if I could stay, although they assumed it was because I was upset about something. After a couple of days I told both Nat and Helen separately what I'd done. Nat's reaction has stayed with me ever since. He said:

'Whenever I look at you I see two things: a girl with an amazing ability to do wonderful and powerful things for God, and a girl with an amazing ability to throw it all away. I see you at a crossroads at the moment, and there are two paths: the first is you in five years' time achieving all those wonderful things that God has in store for you, and the second is you in five years' time dead. And the thing that scares me – that really scares me – is that I can't see anything in between.'

I couldn't speak. Eventually Nat told me he was going to bed and left me sitting in the living room to think. Nat was not the type of person who'd speak before he'd thought about it, and he didn't use shock tactics. I just sat and went through everything he had said in my head and started to cry, because I knew that it was true and entirely from God; and that terrified me. It was a slap in the face that was necessary. That second path, the path of self-destruction, was not something I wanted. I'd never wanted it, but I knew it was a definite possibility if I didn't do something to stop it. I didn't want to die, but I knew I could accidentally if I carried on like this. However, I still didn't feel ready to deal with all the things that I needed to.

When I went back to university, Nat's words to me were swiftly placed in the back of my mind because I received a phone call from Lucy asking me to meet up with her. We had met up a few times while I was at university and we seemed to have an unwritten rule: she knew I would not go to her house by myself, and there was no way I'd invite her to my room, so we'd go shopping or out for a meal. And this is what I suggested. I'd told a friend of mine called Andrew about my relative (although he didn't know which relative) who had abused me when I was younger. When I told him that I was meeting up with her, he insisted that he would come to my room and check up on me afterwards. I was really thankful that Andrew insisted on doing this, because I always felt really nervous and agitated after meeting Lucy.

Whenever Lucy and I met up, she'd try to buy everything I looked at for me. I think it was a guilt offering. She felt bad about our past, but to me it always seemed that she was trying to buy my silence. I hated it because I thought my friends considered me spoilt when I'd come back with so many items. Often I'd try to get rid of them without being wasteful by leaving them outside people's doors as gifts. I'd often done this with little bars of chocolate for friends anyway, so it wasn't unusual. In fact I was known in my college as the 'college fairy'. I tried to conceal who the giver of these gifts was, because I never wanted people to thank me for them. I didn't want any gain from her gifts to me.

Conversely, on this occasion when we went shopping I was feeling greedy. This time, I thought, 'I might as well get as much out of her as possible, as she wants to buy things for me anyway.' By the end of the trip Lucy had bought me a meal at a restaurant, a large bouquet of flowers, a vase to put the flowers in, chocolate, food, a really expensive, beautiful bracelet and... a pack of razor blades. I told her I needed them to shave my legs, but really I was planning to use them to hurt myself.

However, as soon as I got home I felt terrible about all the things she'd bought me. It made me feel cheap and used. When Andrew came round I asked him to take the flowers, vase, chocolate and food, insisting that he mustn't thank me for them. But I deliberately didn't tell him about the bracelet or the razor blades. I was experiencing ambivalent feelings about the bracelet: part of me still loved it, as it was very pretty and I'd admired it from afar for a long time. But now that she'd bought it, this gorgeous trinket was tainted. Andrew stayed with me for a while. I was very fidgety and stressed because I couldn't get Lucy out of my head and I didn't want to be comforted. Andrew could tell I wasn't doing well, so asked if I wanted to go for a walk. I said OK, got my coat and put the bracelet in my pocket.

As we were walking, Andrew asked me what happened when I prayed about 'the relative'. I'd never really prayed about Lucy, apart from that one time with

Bev. I tried to shrug off his question. But Andrew told me it seemed that whenever he tried to mention God within the context of 'the abuser' I closed my ears. I admitted I was aware of this. Then I said something that surprised me:

'If I'm honest, I think it's because I blame him for the things that happened to me when I was young.' I warned Andrew not to go down the line of the 'free will argument' – that in order for us to be able to choose to love God, he has given us the choice to turn away from him also, so he allows us to sin, and it is our choice and not God's fault when we do. I told Andrew I didn't care about the free will argument, because my feelings were irrational, and although I knew the argument made sense I didn't want to hear it.

'OK, be as irrational as you like!' Andrew encouraged.

'I don't care, because "free will" just isn't good enough. And the saying I've heard, that God was crying with me, isn't good enough either. I don't care that he was crying with me. He could have stopped it instead of crying at all. And he didn't... and don't you dare stand up for him!'

I couldn't believe I was saying all this. I didn't realize just how angry I was with God for what had happened to me. I never thought I was. Andrew asked me how God could have stopped it, and I said:

'By telling someone to walk in on me and her. Telling a random Christian who was driving through my town to drive down my road, run into my house and stop her.'

'Don't you think he was?' Andrew replied. 'Don't you think he was shouting at everyone around you, but they wouldn't listen?'

I started crying. I looked at the bracelet. 'He's let me become this,' I said, showing Andrew the bracelet. 'I don't want to be it,' I sighed. 'You know how when you're little you get wishes everywhere?'

'How do you mean?'

'Like, when you blow out the candles on your birthday cake, or when you throw some money down a wishing well, or when you catch fairies, or get an eyelash?'

'Oh, yeah.'

'Well, when I was little I used to wish the same thing every time. I knew that most of my friends were wishing for ice cream or a new toy or things like that, and so because I realized my wish was a lot bigger than that I thought I needed to save them up to make sure they came true.' I chuckled at the thought.

'What did you wish for?' Andrew asked.

'I know it's daft, and it sounds so silly to an adult; but I used to wish I could be an angel. I used to think that angels were great because God loves them. They get to be with him. They have lots of friends. They can do their homework really quickly and everyone else's, so everyone likes them... and angels can fly away. No one can hurt angels, because if things get bad they can just fly away. I mean, I know my theology wasn't perfect in those days, but part of me is still saddened that he didn't answer my prayer.'

I couldn't believe I was being so honest with Andrew. I was telling him things I hadn't allowed myself to think about.

'God didn't answer your prayer, because you're better than an angel,' Andrew said. 'You're his child: why would he want to demote you? God doesn't want you to fly away from your troubles, he wants to lead you through them by the hand.'

I started crying again. I said, 'Look what I've become: this pathetic, damaged whore.' I still didn't want to believe what Andrew was saying. During all this I just kept looking at the bracelet I'd made Lucy buy for me. I wanted her to spend as much money on me as possible, but then when she did I felt even cheaper and didn't want her presents. The more money she spent on me the more devalued I became. This bracelet started to become a thing that represented all of that in my mind.

We continued walking until we got to an old bridge spanning the local river, a stunning beauty spot in the city. We stood on the bridge, looking down at the water in silence. After a while Andrew hesitantly said to me, 'I think you're angry at the wrong person.'

'Oh, no, I'm angry at her too,' I responded bitterly.

He encouraged me to see that I needed to forgive her in time, even though it'd hurt.

'I was two years old!' I shouted. I was so angry that Andrew could think I should forgive someone who could do these things to such a young child.

'I know, and it wasn't your fault. But I think all these presents are her way of trying to make it OK, her way of apologizing.'

Now when I looked down at the bracelet it seemed horrible. I couldn't see any of the loveliness I had seen in it before. She had bought me, she had paid for me, and this thing was my price.

I shouted, partly at Andrew, but mainly at the bracelet:

'So this is what I'm worth? Some pathetic £20 bracelet?' Without thinking, I threw the bracelet I hated into the river, turned round, and would have buckled if Andrew hadn't caught me. It hurt so much, I couldn't even stand.

As he was holding me, Andrew said, 'You're priceless, Sophs, you're a child of God. God was willing to send his Son to die for you because you're so precious. And you're my friend and I think you're priceless too. You just have to realize how much you're worth. If you do that you'll never want to hurt yourself.'

'It's the Devil telling you that somehow because you "lost your innocence" at such a young age you're worthless. If you keep thinking you're worthless, you'll keep allowing other people to treat you badly too.'

Eventually Andrew came back to my room and I gave him all my razor blades, including the ones that Lucy had given me.

It was after speaking with John, Nat and Andrew that I decided to see a counsellor again. I was really worried because of my bad experience with Amy, the counsellor I saw when I was seventeen. But because Nat's words still rang in my head and that 'second option' terrified me more, I went to the university's counselling service and asked to be put on the waiting list to see a counsellor. I specified that I wanted a male counsellor. There were two reasons why I asked for a male one: first because Lucy was female and I knew that my experience with her had left me with some reserve towards women, and secondly because my first counsellor was female and that hadn't worked out. That wasn't to say that I couldn't trust women. Bev, Ruth and Laura, not to mention many other friends I made at university whom I haven't mentioned, had been invaluable to me. It was just that I'd seen how often my closest and most trusting friendships were with guys: Carter, Nat, Tom, John and Andrew. After a few weeks' waiting I received an email telling me that I could meet up with a counsellor called Kevin once a week.

I arrived for the meeting two minutes late and knocked on the office door. The question of when I should turn up had been running through my mind since I'd received the email the week before. I intended to be slightly late because I didn't want Kevin to think I was desperate, but not too late, because I also didn't want him to think I was rude. The secretary answered the door and invited me into a small waiting room. She then called Kevin on an intercom and told him I'd arrived. A moment later the door opened slightly and a man with a friendly face popped his head round the door and said:

'Sophie?' I smiled and stood up. 'Hi, I'm Kevin.' He smiled and shook my hand. 'Do you want to come through?'

We walked across the corridor and into a large room with a fireplace, a desk and two comfy chairs by the window. Kevin asked me to pick a seat and sit down. He then explained what normally happened in a counselling session, the time we'd have – fifty minutes to an hour – to talk about anything I wanted to, and the rules about general confidentiality.

Kevin and I got on incredibly well. He once said that he thought we had the most open counselling relationship he'd ever had. It was a carefully navigated honesty, because I sometimes would not tell him things, although I would be open in my lack of telling. Kevin knew that I had some secrets from my past that I wasn't ready to tell him. I was still worried about telling a counsellor what had happened with Lucy, thanks to my last experience. I also felt ambiguous towards what had happened with her, so I didn't want him to assume automatically that it was sexual abuse. Even though I'd been speaking to Andrew a few weeks before, positive that it was abuse, again I slipped back into thinking it might have been a misunderstanding.

We had many sessions together talking about many things besides my self-harm. I told him how I wanted to work for the church as a youth worker, that I was passionate about young people and wanted to help them in any way I could. We discussed a huge event I was organizing for a thousand young people to get together to worship God. I told him about my friends and how I hated lying to them about things because I loved them so much. We also discussed how I took overdoses sometimes because they didn't leave any visible mark on my skin that I'd have to hide the next day, and that that was the main reason why I'd do that instead of cutting. I told Kevin what Nat had said about ending up dead, and Kevin told me that he was worried that that could happen too. He challenged me that I was risking my health for vanity because cutting myself was much safer than taking overdoses. We eventually agreed that I would stop taking the overdoses, and that if I did feel triggered I could allow myself to cut myself instead. It sounds like a strange thing to decide upon, to start cutting myself again, but it was definitely a step in the right direction.

They were really good but difficult times because they were very emotional and I still found emotions relatively difficult. This meant that during that time my self-harm got worse again to cope with the sessions. I'd also stopped eating again. I'd started competing with myself as to how long I could go without eating a single meal, my longest period being three days. A very negative thing that I'd started to do was to keep a scrapbook of 'thinspiration' to encourage me in my lack of eating. It was full of pictures of models and emaciated women that I'd printed off the internet. I'd also filled it with words describing myself: 'fat', 'worthless', 'damaged goods', 'disgusting', 'dirty', 'pathetic', 'freak' and other spiteful names.

It was during the very last session I had with Kevin that I felt God spoke through him to me. We were both leaving university, and although we felt I still needed some more sessions, it wasn't practical. Because it was our last session, I decided to be honest with him about my scrapbook, and I brought it in with me.

Kevin asked me how I'd been feeling since the previous week. I explained to him that I hadn't been eating and thought I'd been spending an unhealthy amount of time making up my scrapbook. I took it out of my bag and placed it on my lap. The book had a blue and pink silk cover, and was bound on one side and tied together with string on the other.

'Is that the book?' he asked.

I nodded. 'Yes, I've been thinking about showing it to you.' Saying these things to Kevin had always been easy because I never felt any pressure to go any further than I wanted to. I knew I could say I wanted to show him without then having to show him.

'Do you think you can?'

'I'm not sure.'

'OK, well don't feel you have to if you don't want to,' he reassured me. Part of me was really pleased he'd said that, but another part was frustrated because I thought if he'd asked me to hand it over to him I would have done so, and it would have been easier with the pressure.

I stroked the silk with my index finger and weighed up in my mind the positives and negatives of showing Kevin the book. The positives were that it could help me to be honest. It would be a big step for my last session: even if Kevin did react badly I didn't have to see him again. The negatives were that I really liked Kevin and didn't want him to react badly even though I wasn't going to see him again. Eventually I decided the positives outweighed the negatives and without saying anything I handed him my book.

'Thank you,' he said, reaching out to take it. 'Can I read it?'

'Yes,' I said.

Kevin opened the book and I started to worry. He flicked through the book one agonizing page at a time. With every page I tried to remember what I'd written and picture what he was reading, but that made me panic more. I looked away and thought:

'That's it, Sophie. He's lost all respect for you now. He thinks you're completely insane and he might even have you committed, you stupid, stupid girl! Why did you do it?'

When I looked back I saw something I didn't expect: Kevin was crying. I was really shocked because Kevin was a very professional counsellor. I trusted him and knew he wouldn't try to manipulate me. I realized I must have really upset him.

He eventually closed the book and rested it on his lap with one hand on it and looked up at me. I didn't want him to look at me. I was so ashamed. I hid my face in my hands and flinched. He didn't say anything. This time, the silence between us didn't feel comfortable. I didn't know what Kevin was thinking, and this distressed me.

'What on earth are you thinking?' I said through my hands, still not looking up.

'Honestly?' he asked.

I nodded, still not looking up.

'Sophie, honestly, I don't mind you trying to lose weight, I don't mind you keeping a scrapbook to help you do that. I'd prefer if you did it healthily and safely, but that's not what's upset me. What I hate, I really hate, is that you write such horrible things about yourself.'

He paused. I looked up at him and saw he was still crying. He had such an earnest, concerned look on his face.

'It's pure self-destruction, or even, if I can use the term properly, self-abuse.'

That word: abuse. Somehow I'd never seen what I was doing to myself as abuse. I couldn't see it as that big a deal. I'd always managed to convince myself it wasn't anything too bad or major. But abuse? That's a big deal. I started crying too. We both sat in silence again for a while until it was the end of the session.

I was worried that Kevin was going to tell me time was up and that we'd have to end there. I didn't feel able to end like that, with me having made him cry and not really understanding why. But instead of calling time, Kevin asked if he could get a shredder and if I'd shred the book.

'I don't know,' I said. I'd spent hours making my scrapbook and a huge part of me wanted to continue adding to it. The silliest thing is that I was proud of how well presented it was, and didn't want to destroy my handiwork.

'I'm not going to force you, but I think it'd be good,' Kevin encouraged.

I sat there thinking about it for another couple of minutes, then checked the time.

'Don't you need to see your next client?' I was concerned.

'He can wait. This is more important right now,' Kevin assured me.

After about ten more minutes I said OK, and he immediately got up and left the room to get a shredder.

Because the book was bound, I had to tear out all the leaves and shred them one by one. As I was tearing the pages I kept thinking about how I'd made Kevin cry, and what that could mean. Kevin was silent as I shredded, so I turned to him and asked:

'What on earth do you think of me?' I needed to know. I was expecting to hear him say that he thought I was really ill and messed up, and that maybe I shouldn't be a youth worker because I'd do more harm than good. I didn't care how bad his view was, I just had to know what it was.

'Honestly? No beating about the bush?'

'Honestly,' I agreed.

'Because we've been so honest with each other so far, and it's our last session, so we might as well be totally up-front?'

This worried me a little. It made me wonder just how bad his opinion of me could be if he needed to clarify this so much first, but I still needed to know.

'Yes,' I said.

'I think you're lovely. That's it. I think you're really

lovely and I can't understand why you could think so badly of yourself.'

This made me start crying again. I believed him. I trusted that he wouldn't lie to me and this was what he honestly thought. I couldn't understand why he'd think I was lovely, but something inside me wanted to learn why. I wanted to find out if he was right and see if I was lovely.

'Thank you,' I said.

By now we were running half an hour over time, and Kevin received a phone call telling him that the next client was waiting for him. He explained to me that our session had to finish now.

'Thank you so much,' I repeated. 'I mean, thank you for putting up with me and all this stupid stuff.'

'I'd do it all over again, and again and again.'

We both stood up, and as usual Kevin held out his hand for me to shake, which was customary at the end of our sessions. But I said 'No' and gave him a hug instead. I was only planning to give him a very quick hug, as I was worried that it wasn't professional, but when I tried to pull away he carried on holding me. It confirmed to me even more that he honestly did care about me and it wasn't just a charade because he was my counsellor. I thanked him again, and as I left he watched me walk down the corridor and waved to me.

10.

FROM NOW ON

After I left university I started working for a church as a youth worker. I loved working there and felt very supported and cared for. Although the self-harm was still something I occasionally did, the frequency had decreased significantly and the vicar was very understanding and encouraging. I was able to work with children and young people of all ages and even got to take an older group away to Soul Survivor. It was there that God decided it was time for me to finally know the truth about what had happened with Lucy.

During one of the evening sessions I had been praying for others at the front of the arena, away from my youth group. I loved doing this because it felt such a privilege to be with someone and pray for them as they met with God. I'd also recently been praying for the gift of prophecy, and was learning to use it. The vicar at the church I worked for had been encouraging me to pray for this gift for some time and I had started to receive a few words for friends I'd prayed with. So I decided to see if God wanted to use me and this gift with strangers as well. After I'd finished praying with a couple of people, I looked round to find I couldn't see anyone else who needed prayer. I thought I could use this opportunity to pray for myself and ask God again whether what had happened with Lucy was just a misunderstanding or whether it was abuse. Even though I'd told people about her and had even started to use the words 'sexual abuse', I still couldn't believe it myself. I needed to know for sure whether it was or wasn't. So I stood praying alone – although I was surrounded by thousands of people – that God would let me know. I told him I was ready to find out now and that I needed to be told. I waited for what seemed like hours with my hands held out, simply waiting and waiting on God, until eventually I felt two simple words come into my mind: 'It was.'

That was it. Just two words. But with those two words, God had confirmed everything that I didn't want to be true. I knew it wasn't just my mind telling me those words, because I would never allow myself to think that way. I somehow just knew that it was God.

I screamed. I actually screamed. I've never screamed before in my life but I couldn't help myself. I screamed as loud as possible: 'NO!'

It was as if part of me was worried that over the noise of the arena, God might not hear me and my anguish. I fell to my knees and cried. It was all true. I didn't want it to be, but it was. I started to beg God to make it not true, to change it somehow and make it 'un-happen'.

As this was happening, two women came over, laid hands on me and started praying. I kept struggling with God, repeating:

'No, Lord, please, no. Please, please? I don't want it to be true! No, Lord, please.'

However, although I was still begging God to change my entire life, I started to feel completely safe and reassured, even valued. Kevin's expression of care and Andrew's word 'precious' began to make sense.

Things started to seem clearer. It was as if through this disclosure, God had finally lifted a veil that I had put over my own eyes. Now I was able to see things for what they really were. Yes, what Lucy had done to me had really happened. Yes, it was terrible and painful and it shouldn't have happened. But I was still valuable and treasured; it didn't change that. As this realization dawned, I began to feel at peace. I lay on the floor as the two ladies continued praying for me, and steadily allowed myself to feel precious for the first time. Ever.

I'd always found it easier to see myself as valueless, because if that were true it would mean that all the things that happened to me during my childhood didn't matter. It was a coping mechanism that I started to form when I was six years old. That was the time when I decided, 'It hurts to feel like this, so I'll stop feeling it.' That decision caused me to start devaluing myself. It was far easier to see what occurred with Lucy as not a big deal, because it had happened to an insignificant person, than to accept that it was unfair and important to acknowledge. I was living a clever type of denial, whereby I could sometimes accept the incidents as real but could either deny their impact or deny the intention behind them. The reason why I found it hard to say 'sexual abuse' was that the term 'abuse' is a big deal, and there would be no way for me to hide from the reality of it.

The main thing I have learnt through my experiences with self-harm and sexual abuse is to trust in God and his timing. Countless times I'd pray to him for hours for healing and end up feeling disenchanted and frustrated because nothing seemed to change. I would question whether God wanted to heal me and wonder if the reason why he didn't was that there was something wrong with me. I wanted a miraculous 'Pow! Ka-blam! All better!' healing – the type I'd hear in testimonies at Christian festivals or read about in books. I wanted God to take away all the pain that Lucy had caused, to stop any desire I had to hurt myself and also to heal all the scars (or even open wounds) that I had, but this never seemed to happen. However, the truth is, God does heal, and he was (and still is) healing me, only in his own time.

Tori Dante expressed it better than I ever could in her book *Our Little Secret*, when she wrote:

> If God had healed me in an instant I would have not known who I was! I would have had an identity crisis. After all I was the product of years

of pain and trouble that had shaped my life and my reactions, my outlook and my attitudes.

I'd been abused since the age of two; when I was six I'd dramatically changed my outlook on life by stopping myself feeling certain emotions. If God had healed all of that straight away I would no longer have been me. Even though I asked him for it, his immediate healing would have left me feeling mistreated and invaded by God rather than loved and cared for. He knew better than I did that the best way to restore me was slowly and gently.

God encouraged me to walk with him through my past, but he never manipulated me into it. Looking back, it is easy to see him working through my friends, through church members and in the silence, bit by bit, tenderly and lovingly allowing his healing to cleanse me. Andrew and Kevin helped me to understand that I was of real value. I'd always seen myself as worthless, and honestly thought that people were friendly to me only because they were kind and caring, not because they saw any true value in me. I feel that God used others to start transforming my opinion of myself from an insignificant nobody into a loved and appreciated daughter of God.

Slowly, with the understanding that I was accepted, loved and precious in God's sight, I was able to look at my past and start to come to terms with it. There are still times when I find myself denying what happened to me because it is easier, but as I began accepting and dealing with the past, the self-harming incidents decreased. It was a very gradual process and it is one that is still happening now. Together, God and I are working through all the pain, anger and confusion that I have within me. There are times when he has to be very patient and forgiving, but he is gracious enough to stay with me, and I am so thankful to him that he is.

I wish I could end this book by saying that I am sure I will never hurt myself again. But I set out to be completely honest here in order to help others in similar situations, and I feel that if I said that, I'd be giving false hope. The desire to hurt myself is still with me, and it may always be. The trouble with an addiction is that the addict knows that whatever they are addicted to 'works'. It can give them that feeling they are looking for, even if it causes many more problems in the long run. There is a phrase that some alcoholics use to describe their difficulty:

'Once an alcoholic, always an alcoholic, just not always a drunk.'

I may always be a self-harmer, that is, I may always have some amount of desire to hurt myself when things get bad, but that doesn't necessarily mean that I will.

Whenever I start to feel down, or question God's love for me, I try to read a psalm or two. David was a devoted follower of God, but many times he'd write about how he felt God had abandoned him or didn't love him. Yet even though he doubted God, God never gave up on him: in fact God blessed him! I love Psalm

121, as I find it such an encouragement to me to remember who God is:

> I lift up my eyes to the hills –
> where does my help come from?
> My help comes from the Lord,
> the Maker of heaven and earth.
> He will not let your foot slip –
> he who watches over you will not slumber;
> indeed, he who watches over Israel
> will neither slumber nor sleep.
> The Lord watches over you –
> the Lord is your shade at your right hand;
> the sun will not harm you by day,
> nor the moon by night.
> The Lord will keep you from all harm –
> he will watch over your life;
> the Lord will watch over your coming and going
> both now and for evermore.
> Psalm 121

As I've gradually tried to come to terms with my past and understand more of God's grace, my desire to hurt myself has diminished. One day that desire may be so small that it disappears for ever. What I know for sure is that God is good, loving and forgiving, and I know he's never going to give up on me.

APPENDIX

Helpful websites and phone numbers.

Bodies Under Siege (bus)

www.buslist.org/phpBB/index.php

Bus is a safe, on-line community of self-harmers and their friends and family. It is for those who are recovered, in recovery, wanting to be in recovery or not yet ready to stop. It provides important information about self-harm, but is also a place where harmers can go to feel encouraged, supported and cared for by other harmers. There are strict rules about posting anything that may trigger others.

ChildLine

www.childline.org.uk

Tel: 0800 11 11

ChildLine is the UK's free, 24-hour helpline for children in distress or danger. Trained volunteer counsellors comfort, advise and protect children and young people who may feel they have nowhere else to turn.

The Lantern Project

www.victimsnolonger.org.uk

The Lantern Project is a charity and website set up to support victims of childhood sexual abuse.

Mind (National Association for Mental Health)
www.mind.org.uk
Mind is a charity that provides information and support, and campaigns to improve policy and attitudes. It also provides informative leaflets about self-harm which are issued on request.

National Self Harm Network
www.nshn.co.uk
The National Self Harm Network is a survivor-led organization committed to campaigning for the rights and understanding of people who self-harm. It provides facts about self-harm, resources and forums for professionals and family members.

NSPCC (National Society for the Prevention of Cruelty to Children)
www.nspcc.org.uk
If you are worried that a child is being abused or neglected, the NSPCC provides a 24-hour Child Protection Helpline:
Tel: 0808 800 5000

One in Four
www.oneinfour.org.uk
One in Four is run for and by people who have experienced sexual abuse and sexual violence. The reason for the title is that it is estimated that one in four children will experience some form of sexual abuse before they reach eighteen.

The Samaritans
www.thesamaritans.org.uk
Email: jo@samaritans.org
Tel: 08457 90 90 90
Samaritans is available 24 hours a day to provide confidential emotional support for people who are experiencing feelings of distress or despair, including those which may lead to suicide.

Self Harm

www.selfharm.org.uk

This site is an information resource for young people who self-harm, their friends and families, and professionals working with them.

There 4 me

www.there4me.com

There4me is for people age 12–16 who are worried about something and need some help. It is there for people struggling with issues such as abuse, bullying, exams, drugs and self-harm.

Contact

If you would like to contact Sophie Scott, you can email her at the following address:
Sophs.Scott@gmail.com